made
at home

a guide to simple sewing

by **lisa stickley**

**NORTH
LIGHT
BOOKS**
Cincinnati, Ohio

this book is dedicated to auntie linda.
for her unwavering passion for life and
love, her support, and her wonderfully
colorful dresses.

editorial director jane o'shea
creative director helen lewis
project editor lisa pendreigh
designer claire peters
photographer ben anders
stylist katie sellers
illustrator lisa stickley
production director vincent smith
production controller ruth deary

published in the United States by
North Light Books
a division of F+W Media, Inc.
4700 East Galbraith Road
Cincinnati, Ohio 45236
(800) 289-0963
First Edition.

14 13 12 11 10   5 4 3 2 1

media
www.fwmedia.com

ISBN-13: 978-1-4403-0912-0

british library cataloguing-in-publication data
a catalog record for this book is available from the
british library.

printed in china.

it probably started with lego, but for as long as i can remember, i have always been making, creating, painting, and drawing—everything from cupcakes with fluffy frosting to hand-cut paper flowers and wooden picture frames (using all of dad's scraps from the shed). in our house *the reader's digest family book of things to make and do* from the 1970s was well used.

for a while my mother used to make some of her own clothes and mine, but it was my auntie daphne that i spent most of my sewing and knitting time with at an early age. on saturdays, my mother, my auntie daph, and i made regular morning shopping trips, returning armed with gooey cakes to spend the afternoon making things.

i learned a lot from both my mother and my auntie. in my early teens i was given a hand-turning sewing machine and then, just before starting my college degree, i acquired an electric one. while i trained professionally as a printed textile designer, i have never specifically had any formal training in dressmaking or pattern cutting. i just have a great passion for creating and with a lot of practice have learned that, with some simple techniques and an ability to stitch two layers of fabric together, you can create some beautiful and often very useful items.

as with cooking, it is important to start with good "ingredients." handsome items can be made using the simplest of techniques, but will look absolutely stunning if the fabric you start with is good quality. this doesn't mean you need to spend a fortune on lavishly expensive fabrics, you just need to keep an eagle eye out for the diamonds in the rough and search out pieces you love and those suitable for the project in hand.

the idea of this book is to share my passion for homemaking; if you have even just an ounce of desire to be creative, i hope that *made at home* will give you the inspiration and confidence to make some items for yourself. we are not talking couture—intricately detailed and fabulously expensive finished products—but lovely handmade items for you and your own home. things that will brighten and smarten up your rooms, add an original, personal touch, and be used and loved for all their (perhaps slightly imperfect) perfection.

when writing the instructions for this book (which did result in more than a few very late nights with quill and desk lamp!) i have tried my best to be as clear and straightforward as i can. there is a mixture of projects throughout, ranging from easy to slightly more challenging. as with most things it is much easier when you know how, so i would encourage you to stick the radio on, have a cup of coffee at the ready, and have a go. as they say, practice makes perfect and the main thing is to enjoy the process!

happy sewing,

lisa.

basics

fabrics and basic equipment.

i have suggested specific weights and types of fabrics for each project. below are descriptions of some familiar fabrics to help you choose what to use. different fabrics produce different end results; all i would say is that if the ingredients are good, the item you are making will be all the better for it.

fabrics

plain weave the most basic form of textile weave—also referred to as taffeta, canvas, or duck—is most readily available in cotton, silk, and wool (among others). a hardwearing fabric; the heavier weights are great for upholstery and the medium weights for home furnishings.

denim a heavyweight fabric, often indigo-dyed, most obviously used for jeans. constructed in a diagonal weave, it is extremely hardwearing. ideal for footstools and doorstops.

twill like denim, twill has a characteristic diagonal weave. available in cotton, wool, and silk in light and medium weights, examples are chino, drill, tweed, and serge. a great fabric for many projects in this book. in a beautiful medium-weight cotton, linen, or silk, twill is perfect for pillows and shades.

canvas a heavyweight fabric that, like denim, is extremely strong. in a beautiful linen this can be stunning and is perfect for heavy-duty projects where sturdiness is required.

satin or sateen, woven in either cotton or silk. with a glossy, luxurious finish, satin is more commonly used for garments. i used it for the pin-tucked pillow (see pages 110–13) where it gave a wonderful finish. but unless you are well practiced, i recommend cotton satin rather than silk, as it can be tricky to handle.

taffeta a plain woven fabric, most commonly in silk, of which there are two distinct types: piece-dyed taffeta and yarn-dyed taffeta. the former is much softer and more suitable for linings, with the latter being much stiffer. often used for wedding dresses, this deluxe fabric lends itself beautifully to draperies and pillows.

muslin an unbleached plain cotton weave available in light, medium, and heavy weights. sometimes it is not fully processed but also available as preshrunk. used in the fashion industry for "toiles" (mock-up garments), muslin is great to practice with as it is cheap. it also serves well as a sturdy lining.

herringbone weave a distinctive v-shaped pattern most commonly produced in wool for suiting, this cloth is also hardwearing and a good option for many interior projects.

damask available in endless patterns, the designs are woven into the cloth rather than printed. available in silk, wool, linen, cotton, or synthetics, a wonderful fabric for home projects.

brocade very similar in process to the damask above, brocade has a raised pattern woven into the fabric to give the appearance of an embroidered finish. classic luxury at its best.

dupion silk a silk with a subtle textured crisp finish and a glorious sheen. wonderful for pillows and lightweight curtains.

tasar silk this softer silk is a good medium to heavyweight fabric; perfect for a number of home projects. i used this for the winter curtain (see pages 80–5) and it gave a great finish.

equipment

the main items you will need are illustrated opposite, but there are always other useful bits and pieces that can be added to your toolbox as and when you need them:
large sheets of paper, old newspaper
tailor's chalk
curved needles (light and upholstery-weight)
masking tape
seam ripper
thread snips
cotton bias binding – ½ in (12mm), ¾ in (2cm) and 1 in (2.5cm) wide
polyester batting

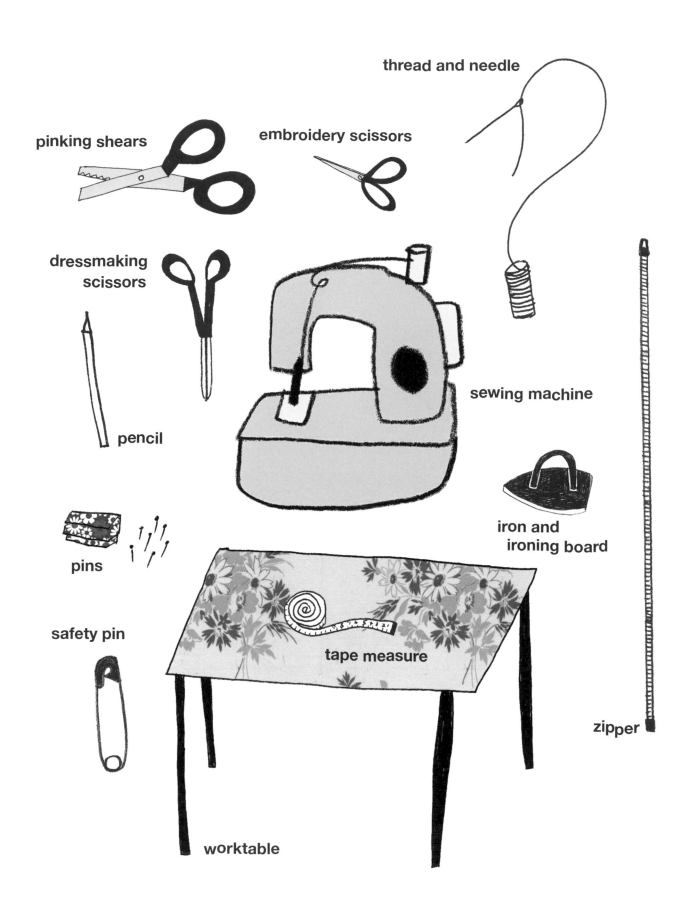

thread and needle

pinking shears

embroidery scissors

dressmaking scissors

pencil

sewing machine

iron and ironing board

pins

safety pin

tape measure

zipper

worktable

fabrics and basic equipment **11**

stitches.

although not all of these stitches have been mentioned throughout the projects in the book, they are important basic skills needed when sewing, and are useful to know. you can dip in and out of this chapter as you work through the projects and perfect your skills with the nuts and bolts of sewing.

small backstitch

when hand sewing you need to fasten the thread at the beginning and end of the stitching with a small backstitch. this is much neater than simply knotting the thread. sew a small initial stitch making sure not to pull the thread right through the fabric, then sew over two or three times more to fasten the thread in place.

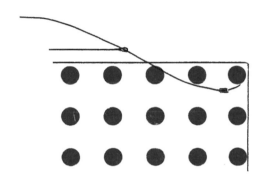

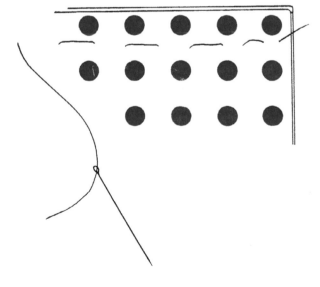

basting

basting is a temporary stitch, which is longer than normal, with the stitches usually around ⅜– ¾in (1–2cm) in length. it is used in many sewing projects and can be an alternative to pinning. the thread from the basting stitch is removed once the fabrics have been machine stitched together (it's helpful to use a contrast color thread for easy removal). this stitch is particularly useful for larger projects such as winter curtains or bedspreads. to stitch two or three pieces of fabric together take your needle and a short length of thread 20in (50cm) should do—and begin at one end with a small backstitch. stitching from right to left, push the needle right the way through the fabric and back toward you in one movement. repeat this along the edge of the fabric with stitches roughly ⅜in (1cm) long, about ⅛in (3mm) from the final seam line. pull the stitches reasonably taut but not too tight as they will need to be removed once the seam has been machine stitched. fasten at the end with a small backstitch.

slipstitch

slipstitch is regularly used for hemming and sewing the side seams in curtains, and other projects where the aim is to achieve an almost invisible stitch on the front side of the fabric. it is very helpful indeed to have a suitably sharp needle for this. with the prepared hem turned, pressed, and ready, and holding the fabric with the wrong side facing and the seam at the top, begin with a secure backstitch in the turned hem. sewing from right to left and keeping the stitches as evenly spaced as you can, push the needle through the turned hem and carefully pick up two or three strands of the facing fabric on its wrong side. the idea is that the thread is only visible as a small point on the front side of the fabric. having brought the needle back through to the wrong side, run it along the hem for ¼in (6mm) then repeat the stitch. repeat this along the length of the hem and secure with a small backstitch to finish.

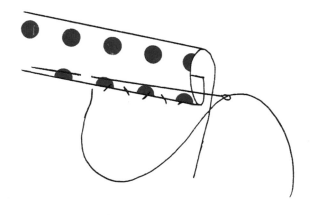

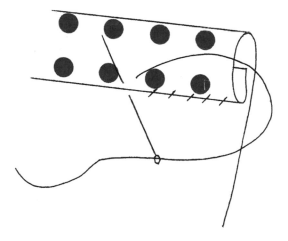

hemming stitch

this is very similar in purpose to the slipstitch and has the same aim—to achieve an almost invisible stitch on the front side of the fabric. with the same method of picking up only two or three threads from the wrong side of the front fabric, make small diagonal stitches along the hem as neatly and evenly as possible, and fasten the thread at the start and finish with a small backstitch.

gathering stitch

gathering stitch is designed to do exactly what the name suggests: gather up fabric, when an article requires it, for example a curve on a valance or fitting a shoulder on a sleeve. for extra strength two parallel rows can be made about $\frac{1}{8}$in (3mm) apart, on either the right or wrong side of the fabric. start with a small backstitch to fasten the thread, then run the needle in and out several times before pulling the needle through, making each stitch around $\frac{1}{8}$in (3mm) long. continue this along the length of the fabric. repeat for the parallel row if necessary, making sure that stitches in the second row line up with the equivalent stitches in the first row. pull up the threads together and wind around a pin to hold in place.

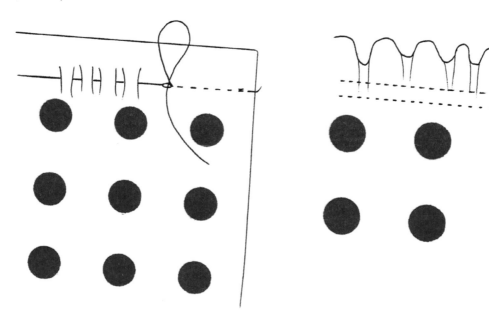

backstitch

this is the hand-sewn equivalent to machine stitching and is very strong, so is generally used when fitting zippers by hand or stitching when there are too many layers of fabric to go through the machine. start with a small backstitch to fasten the thread and make the first stitch from front to back around ¼in (6mm), finishing with the needle to the front in one movement; pull up the thread. go back ⅛in (3mm) to fill in the gap then repeat with the next ¼in (6mm) long stitch. continue this as far as required; the aim is to make a continuous line of thread on both sides of the fabric.

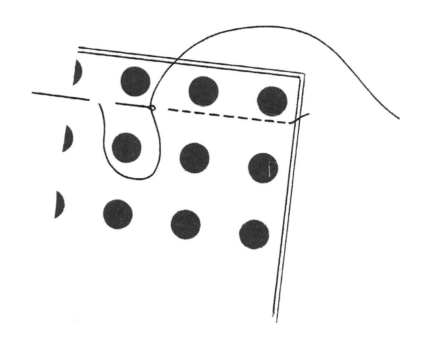

blanket stitch

this stitch is designed to join two pieces of fabric together while creating a decorative stitch along the edge of the fabric at the same time. starting with a small backstitch to secure, take the needle through the fabric from front to back around ¼in (6mm) from the fabric edge. hold the thread under the point of the needle and pull the needle through forming a loop. pull the thread just taut (but not too tight) up to the edge of the fabric and continue, keeping the stitch as even as possible to give a nice finish. fasten with a small backstitch at the end.

seams.

a couple of essential seaming
methods to get you started.

plain seam

this seam is used to join two pieces
of fabric together using a single line of
stitching, far enough from the raw edges
to prevent the fabric from unraveling.
generally a seam of ⅜in–⅝in (1cm–
1.5cm) is recommended. with the two
pieces right sides together, either pin or
tack along the line you are going to stitch
and then machine the seam, securing with
a backstitch at the start and finish. on the
wrong side open out the seam and press
flat to give a neat finish. if you need to
secure the seam (known as a topstitched
seam) then press both allowances to one
side and stitch through all layers of the
seam allowance from the right side, ⅛in
(3mm) from the first stitching.

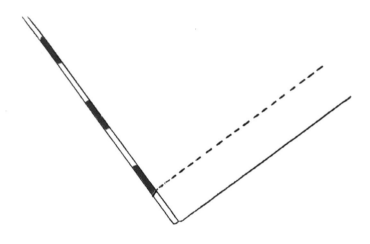

french seam

this seam is generally used for finer fabrics with a tendency to ravel, for example sheer or unlined curtains. also it is a seam commonly used when making shirts, blouses, and other delicate garments. its purpose is to trap the raw edge of the fabric within itself and is therefore not suitable for more heavy-weight fabrics. with the wrong sides of the fabrics together, pin and stitch a ¼in (6mm) seam. trim any raveling edges and press the seam fully out with the right sides together. pin and stitch a second seam, this time ½in (12mm) wide enclosing the raw edges as you sew. this requires a ¾in (18mm) seam allowance. to sew a french seam when the seam allowance is only ⅝in (1.5cm), first stitch a ¼in (6mm) seam, then trim that seam to ⅛in (3mm) and stitch a ⅜in (9mm) second seam.

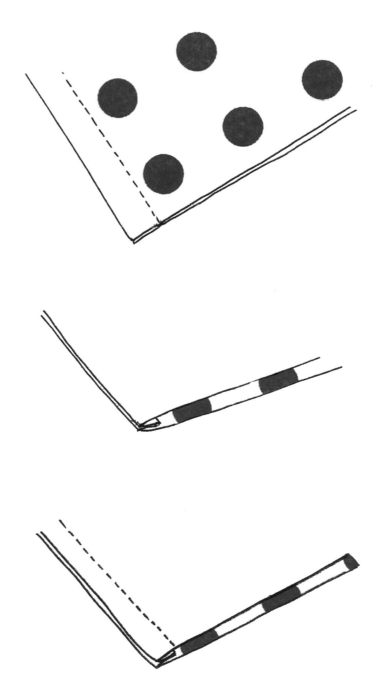

corners and curves.

useful tips to help you tackle corners
and curves with neatness and ease.

turned corners

when stitching a corner
and before turning to right
side out, trim the seam
allowance diagonally
across the corner to
achieve a neat finish: a
good technique to use
when making square
pillows, placemats, and
laundry bags.

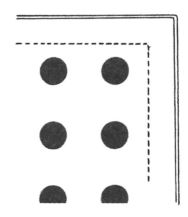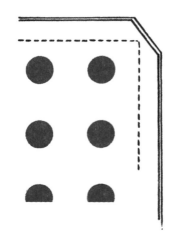

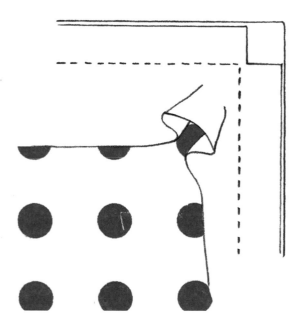

boxed corners

a useful technique to use when making
the outdoor cushion or similar. just
before you reach the corner point cut into
the seam allowance at right angles to the
seam. complete stitching up to this point
and reinforce the corner with a few back
stitches across the diagonal. continue to
stitch the seam down the other edge and
repeat on the following corners.

clipping corners and curves

clipping simply means making small
regular cuts in the raw seam allowance
to help achieve neater corners or curves.
clips reduce the bulk of the fabric when
corners are turned right side out, and
allow the fabric to lie flat when a stitched
curve would otherwise pull it out of shape.

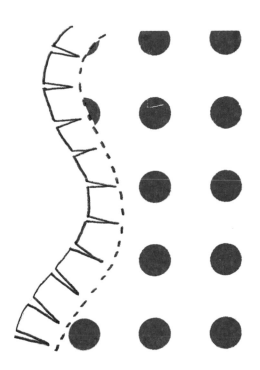

finishes.

some basic techniques and
additional attractive finishes
useful for any number of projects.

bias binding
fold the bias binding lengthwise and pin
in place over the raw edge of the fabric.
stitch as close to the turned-under edge
of the binding as possible, taking care to
catch the underside of the binding as you
sew. tuck the raw edge of the binding
under for a neat finish at each end, and
backstitch the start and finish to secure
the seam.

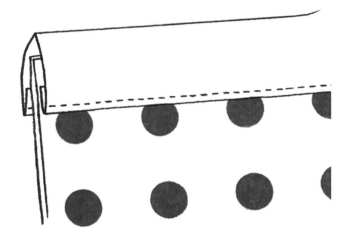

pinking
this is a technique to
prevent a seam from
raveling simply by cutting
along the raw edge of the
seam with pinking shears.

piping

various types of ready-made piping are available from good notions departments, but you can prepare your own using binding and cord. simply wrap the binding around the cord and stitch down the length of the binding as close to the cord as possible with the raw edges lined up. to stitch piping into a cushion or pillow, baste it to the right side of the cushion top or bottom, along the edge, with the piping facing inward and the stitching just inside the stitching line within the seam allowance. use the zipper foot on the machine to help you sew close to the cord. clip into the piping seam allowance at corners and on curves. if you are working on a square pillow it is a good idea to make the corners slightly rounded, which helps the piping sit flat against the fabric. for a neat finish at the ends, trim the cords of the piping (leaving the casing intact) so they butt up against each other and tuck the raw edges of the casing under themselves. to finish the cushion, baste the other piece of the cushion in place, right sides together, and machine all layers together all the way around (be sure to keep the zipper half open so you can turn the cushion right side out when finished! an easy thing to forget... i have done this many a time!).

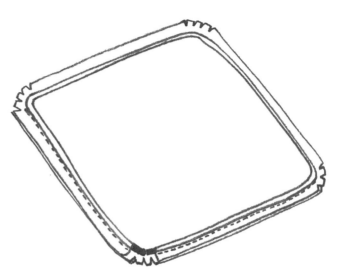

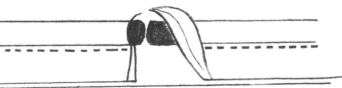

applying a zipper.

a simple method of applying a zipper. it may look a touch daunting but practice on some odds and ends. you will see it's easy once you know how.

a neat way to finish the end of a zipper is to add a zipper end. this is simply a small piece of fabric, 1¼in x 1½in (3cm x 4cm), which will cover the raw end of the zipper. place the small zipper end piece and the cut end of the zipper right sides together. machine in place with a ⅜in (1cm) seam. fold the unstitched side of the zipper end back ⅜in (1cm), then fold the whole piece around to the back side of the zipper being careful to keep the raw edge tucked underneath. machine in place sewing a little to the right of the first seam just sewn, being sure to catch the tucked side of the zipper end in as you stitch.

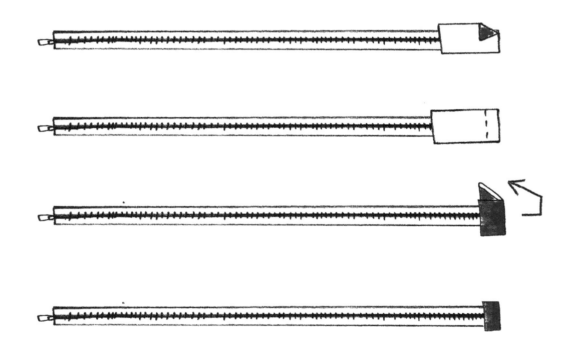

prepare the two pieces of fabric the zipper is to be fitted to by folding and pressing a ⅜in (1cm) hem along the edge of each panel. change over to the zipper foot on your machine. starting with one panel, line the pressed edge of the panel up with the open end of the zipper. i find this easier to machine without pinning in place and with the zipper open by only about ¾in (2cm). depending on the type of zipper foot you have on your machine, it is often easiest to stitch the panel to the zipper with the fabric on the left of the zipper, then turn the zipper around to attach the second panel. a little practice is always handy, so if you have a spare zipper lying around, then this is a great time to have a go with a scrap of fabric to get your confidence up! machine the zipper in place, being sure to backstitch at the start and finish to secure the seam. repeat this on the opposite side of the zipper, this time machining the other panel in place. make sure you line the panels up with each other, and the open end of the zipper.

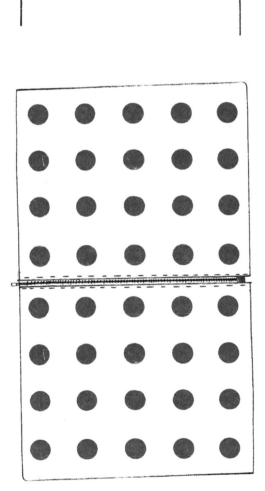

applying a zipper   **23**

buttonholes.

an extremely useful technique to master. the trick is to be patient when stitching by hand. also do not pull the thread too tight—regular, taut, neat stitches are what you are after.

to create a buttonhole by hand

you will need to cut a slit in the fabric in the position required; the slit needs to be the width of the button you are using. you will then need a strong thread to secure your buttonhole with buttonhole stitch, ideally matching the color of the thread to the fabric you are working on. buttonhole stitch is similar to blanket stitch but sewn so the stitches butt up against each other. fasten the thread to start and then take the needle through the fabric from back to front, around ¼in (6mm) from the fabric edge (although this may vary depending on the thickness of the fabric). before you pull the thread taut, loop it around the point of the needle. the aim is to form a knot on the raw edge of the fabric. continue this all the way around the buttonhole until you have created a secure, sealed, neatly stitched hole.

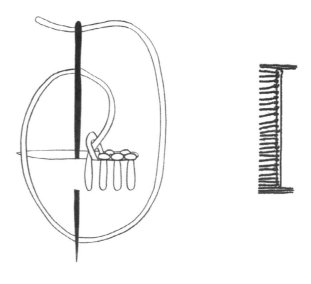

to create a buttonhole with your sewing machine

you will require a special buttonhole foot. if your sewing machine has this then it should also come with simple instructions to follow. as these instructions vary from machine to machine, it is tricky for me to explain the buttonhole technique in detail. the general principle, however, is the same in terms of the size of buttonhole to be made; the only exception is that you machine stitch around the buttonhole before cutting the slit.

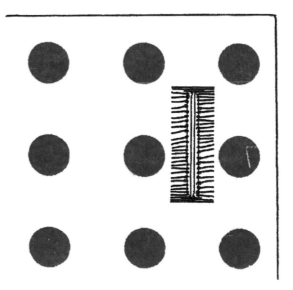

quilting.

quilting is one of the oldest household
crafts; it is a method of holding two layers
of fabric together, with a third layer—
usually batting—in between for extra
warmth.

it is a technique that has been practiced
for hundreds of years and, alongside
patchwork, is celebrated all over the
world, with museums and galleries
displaying examples of this highly
skilled and varied craft. many ladies
(and I am sure gentlemen too) indulge
in the process, creating stunning and
sometimes intricate works that can only
be produced with passion and patience.

simpler quilting techniques, such as that
described on pages 114–17, can be used
to create lovely items. if the fabrics used
are well selected and elegantly luxurious,
with a relatively easy process and a little
time and effort you can make a quilt to be
proud of. if you find the bulk of the fabric
too great to fit under the arm of your
sewing machine, the three layers of fabric
and batting can be stitched together by
hand, but for a small bedspread with a
simple grid pattern and some crafty use
of fabric rolling, the quilting technique
should be achievable on the machine.
once the fabric is basted in place, work
from the outer edge to stitch the first rows
of the grid, rolling the fabric as you go
until you reach the center. repeat on the
opposite side to complete, meeting in the
center. turn the bedspread by 90 degrees
and repeat the process until the whole
grid is finished.

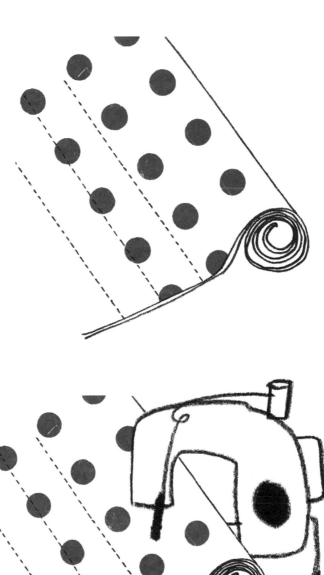

for the **kitchen**

napkins.

things you need

per napkin: 1 piece of medium weight cotton or linen fabric, approximately 20in x 20in (50cm x 50cm) for a regular size napkin.

this is a guide. the same method will easily work for a rectangular napkin—for example, 24in x 16in (60cm x 40cm)—or for a dinky afternoon tea napkin—for example, 12in x 12in (30cm x 30cm)—and pretty much any other size within this arena!

napkins can be made in a variety of sizes and from many different types of cotton or linen. to me they are essential to every meal and i feel lost without one. they are very easy to make and can be coordinated to style your table for a tremendously terrific tea! i like to mix and match, so for a relaxed supper i regularly use an eclectic collection of vintage plates with mismatched linens. for a smarter, more formal dinner i might use something similar to the napkins shown here.

hem the napkin.

fold a ⅜in (1cm) hem over to the wrong side along each edge of the fabric piece and press. repeat this all the way around for a second time so the raw edge of the fabric is concealed. take care not to pull the fabric out of shape and to make neat corners as you press. pin in place then stitch all the way around, sewing as close to the inside edge of the turned hem as possible. backstitch at the start and finish to fasten the seam.

stitch the buttonhole.

for an extra-posh napkin it is a nice touch to add a buttonhole to one corner. i saw this done on a boac airliner napkin from the 1960s; it is a great idea, especially when wearing a white shirt and eating spaghetti! the buttonhole needs to be big enough to fit over a shirt button— approximately ⅝in (1.5cm). the napkin can then be secured neatly to the top button of a shirt, offering maximum protection from bolognese splashes. see page 24 for how to add a buttonhole.

⅜in (1cm)

placemats.

things you need

per placemat: 2 pieces of medium weight cotton, approximately 17in x 13¼in (43cm x 34cm).

whether an intimate dinner for two to a weekend family gathering for twelve, it is a favorite task of mine to set the table. alongside napkins, bread-and-butter plates, water and wine glasses, knives, forks, spoons, salt and pepper pots, vintage candle holders, and pretty flowers, placemats are an essential part of every table setting. they mark your guests' territory at the table and provide a great starting point to plonk all the other bits and pieces around and about them. they are also rather good at protecting your table!

stitch the seams.

place the front and back panels with right sides together. pin around three sides. on the fourth side pin 2¼in (6cm) in from each end, leaving a nice gap through which to turn the placemat right side out when stitched. stitch a ⅜in (1cm) seam where you have pinned. backstitch at the start and finish to fasten the seam. trim the corners (see page 18), then turn the placemat right side out.

close the opening.

press the seams neatly where you have stitched. to finish the open side turn the raw edges under and press so they are level with the stitched edge. stitch the opening, stitching as close to the edge as possible for a neat finish. backstitch at the start and finish to fasten the seam.

bon appetit!

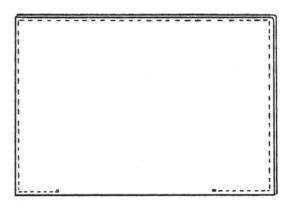

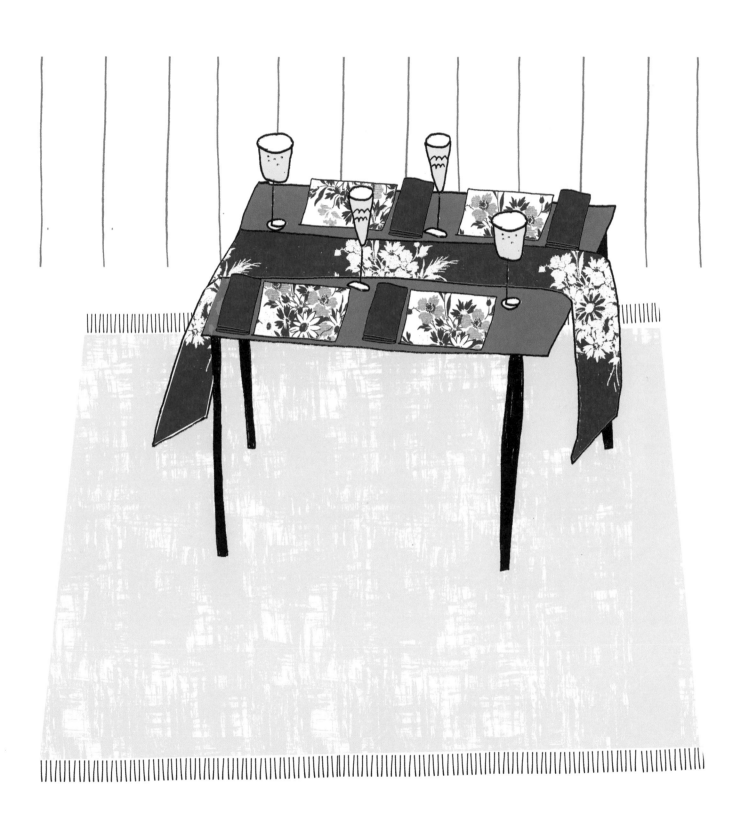

table runner.

things you need

1 piece of medium weight cotton or linen, approximately 14in (34cm) by the length of your table plus 34in (84cm).

the table runner is a neat addition to the dining table, omitting the need for a full tablecloth. combined with placemats, napkins, eclectic china, and stemware, a runner lends an air of sophistication to the modern table. the finished size of the runner obviously depends on the size of your table, but a guide for an average-size dining table is a width of 12in (30cm) or thereabout, with an overhang at either end of 16in (40cm) or so.

hem the table runner.

fold a ⅜in (1cm) hem over to the wrong side along each edge of the fabric piece and press. repeat this all the way around for a second time so the raw edge of the fabric is concealed. pin in place. stitch all the way around, stitching as close to the inside edge of the turned-under hem as possible for a neat finish. backstitch at the start and finish to fasten the seam.

tea cozy.

things you need

1 large sheet of paper or newspaper.

2 semicircular pieces of medium weight cotton for main body (i have used a damask).

2 semicircular pieces of lightweight cotton for lining.

1 rectangular piece of cotton for loop, 1½in x 4in (4cm x 10cm) or thereabouts.

2 semi-circular pieces of 4oz polyester batting for insulation.

tea, cake, and a little herbie hancock on the radio in the background are all particular favorites of mine. this is a nice, easy project to ensure that your tea will be steamy hot even after the cake is gone!

cut out the pieces.
to make sure the cozy fits, lay your teapot on its side on a large piece of paper. draw a semicircle around the teapot adding an extra 2in (5cm) on all sides to make the pattern for the main body and lining. to cut out an even shape, fold the semicircle down the center lengthwise and use the best drawn line as the cutting guide. using this pattern, cut out the fabric for the main body and lining. cut the batting 1½in (4cm) smaller than the pattern all the way around.

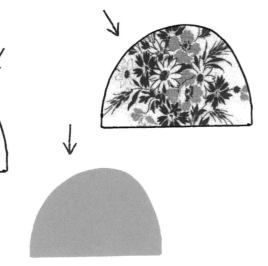

make the loop.

fold a ⅜in (1cm) hem over to the wrong side along each long edge of the fabric piece and press. then fold the fabric in half lengthwise so the two folded edges meet. press and pin. stitch along the open side, stitching as close to the edge as possible for a neat finish. backstitch at the start and finish to fasten the seam. stitch the same line along the opposite side to finish the loop.

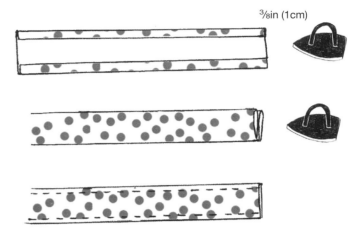

make the main body.

place the two main body pieces right sides together. fold the prepared loop in half and sandwich it between the two main body pieces at the center top, with the raw edges of the loop in line with the raw edges of the main body. pin in place. pin the two body pieces together along the curved edge. stitch together with a ¼in (5mm) seam, catching the loop into the seam as you sew. fold a ⅜in (1cm) hem over to the wrong side around the base and press, but don't stitch this just yet. turn the tea cozy right side out.

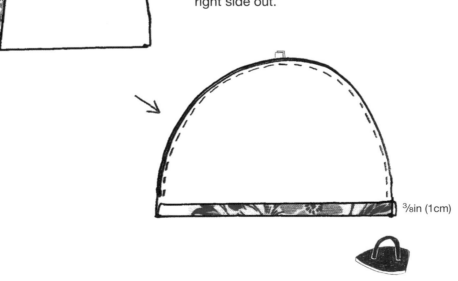

make the lining.
place the two lining pieces right sides together. pin in place along the curved edge. stitch together with a ¼in (5mm) seam. press. fold a ¾in (2cm) hem over to the wrong side around the base and press, but don't stitch this just yet.

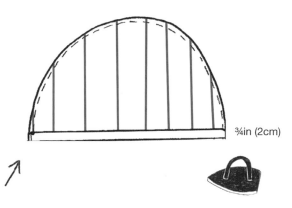

¾in (2cm)

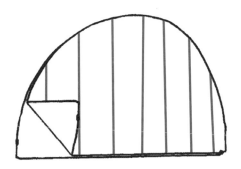

finish the tea cozy.
with wrong sides together slot the lining inside the main body. on each side sandwich a cut piece of batting in between the main body and lining and flatten into place. pin the base of the main body to the lining, making sure the pressed hems are neatly lined up and any stray batting is tucked in. stitch the base together all the way around, stitching as close to the edge of the hem as possible for a neat finish.

put the kettle on for a cup of tea, and i recommend a generous slice of angel cake!

egg cozy.

1 sheet of graph paper with a 2in (5cm) square grid (or hand draw a grid in pencil onto plain paper if you can't find any graph paper).

1 piece of medium weight cotton or lightweight linen for main body; 12in x 12in (30cm x 30cm) is plenty.

1 piece of medium weight cotton for lining; 12in x 12in (30cm x 30cm) is plenty.

1 rectangular piece of cotton for loop, 1½in x 3in (4cm x 8cm) or thereabouts.

2 semicircular pieces of 4oz polyester batting for insulation; 12in x 12in (30cm x 30cm) is plenty.

a selection of newspapers and two soft-cooked eggs with buttered toast are the ingredients for my perfect sunday morning. here is a lovely way to keep your eggs cozy while you make the coffee.

cut out the pieces.

using the template on page 138, cut out a paper pattern for the main body and lining. using this pattern, cut out the fabric for the main body and lining. cut the batting 1½in (4cm) smaller than the template all the way around.

make the loop.

fold a ⅜in (1cm) hem over to the wrong side along each long side of the fabric piece and press. then fold the fabric in half lengthwise so the two folded edges meet. press and pin. stitch along the open side, stitching as close to the edge as possible for a neat finish. backstitch at the start and finish to fasten the seam. stitch the same line along the opposite side to finish the loop.

make the main body.

place the two main body pieces right sides together. fold the prepared loop in half and sandwich it between the two layers at the center top, with the raw edges of the loop in line with the raw edges of the main body. pin in place. pin the two body pieces together along the curved edge. stitch together with a ¼in (5mm) seam, catching the loop into the seam as you sew. backstitch at the start and finish to fasten the ends of the seams. turn right side out and press. fold a ⅜in (1cm) hem over to the wrong side around the base and press.

make the lining.

place the two lining pieces right sides together. pin in place around the curved edge. stitch together with a ¼in (5mm) seam. backstitch at the start and finish to fasten the ends of the seams. press. fold a ⅜in (1cm) hem over to the wrong side around the base and press.

finish the egg cozy.

on each side sandwich a batting piece in between the main body and lining and flatten into place. pin the base of the main body to the lining, making sure the pressed hems are neatly lined up and any stray batting is tucked in. stitch the base together all the way around, stitching as close to the edge of the hem as possible. backstitch at the start and finish to fasten the seam. this bit can be a little tricky on such a tiny item, but with a little patience and practice you will have egg cozies galore.

chef's apron.

things you need

heavyweight cotton canvas cut to size (see template on page 139).

4½yd (4m) of bias binding, 1in (2.5cm) wide, in a contrast color.

2 pieces of tape cotton webbing for side ties, each 48in (120cm) long.

2 pieces of tape cotton webbing for neck ties, each 25½in (65cm) long.

protect your blouse in the most stylish fashion while baking, kneading, whisking, roasting, or any other foodie-related tasks in the kitchen. with ties at both the neck and sides, this is a one-size-fits-all apron and is easy to make too.

add the bias binding.

starting on one straight side, pin the bias binding all the way around the main apron piece. to start each length of binding turn the raw edge under by ⅜in (1cm). as you reach the corners cut the binding with a ⅜in (1cm) excess and tuck this under to conceal the raw edge and give a neat finish. stitch the binding in place all the way around, taking care to catch the bias binding on both sides as you sew. backstitch at the start and finish to fasten the seam.

make the ties.

at each end fold a ⅜in (1cm) hem over twice. stitch a line to secure the ends and prevent raveling. on the wrong side position each tie at either the neck edges or top of each straight side, 2in (5cm) in from the edge of the main apron piece. pin in place. stitch the ties; for extra strength stitch a rectangle and then add a cross in the middle.

now bake a cake to test the apron!

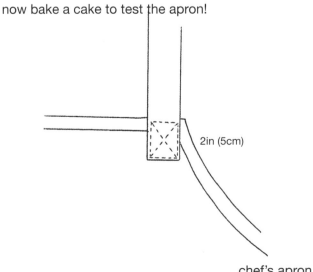

2in (5cm)

half-apron.

things you need

1 piece of lightweight cotton or linen, approximately 21in x 24½in (54cm x 62cm).

1 piece of contrast cotton fabric for the tie, approximately 3in x 60in (8cm x 150cm).

to protect your lower half when performing lighter kitchen duties or to simply assist when lots of hand wiping is called for, this neat little half-apron is the perfect addition to any kitchen.

hem the apron.

fold a ⅜in (1cm) hem over to the wrong side along the bottom edge and both sides of the fabric piece and press. repeat this for a second time so the raw edge of the fabric is concealed. pin in place. stitch the three sides, stitching as close to the inside edge of the hem as possible for a neat finish. backstitch at the start and finish to fasten the seam. fold the fabric piece in half to find the center and mark this point with a pin at the top raw edge.

make the tie.

fold a ⅜in (1cm) hem over to the wrong side along each edge and press. then fold the fabric in half lengthwise so the two folded edges meet and press to make a crease. taking care to keep the pressed crease sharp, unfold the tie. next find the center point of the tie and mark with a pin. position the main body piece and the tie together, matching up the central pins and placing the main body piece just below the pressed crease of the tie.

1cm

make the pleats.

at the marked center of the main body piece make a ⅜in (1cm) pleat. then make another ⅜in (1cm) pleat either side of this first pleat, leaving a 2¼in (6cm) gap between them. press and pin the pleats in place as you go, making sure the pin heads are aiming downward so they are still visible once the top half of the tie is folded down. fold the top half of the tie down to cover the pleated top edge of the main body. pin in place along the entire length of the tie.

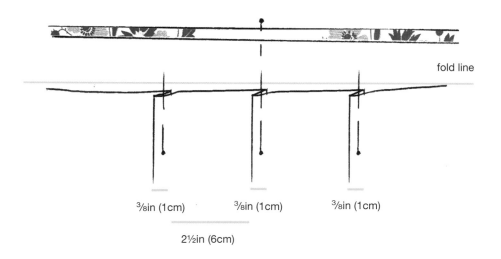

fold line

⅜in (1cm)   ⅜in (1cm)   ⅜in (1cm)

2½in (6cm)

sew it all together.

starting at one end of the tie, stitch all the way along the pinned edge, taking care to enclose the pleated main body as you sew. backstitch at the start and finish to fasten the stitch.

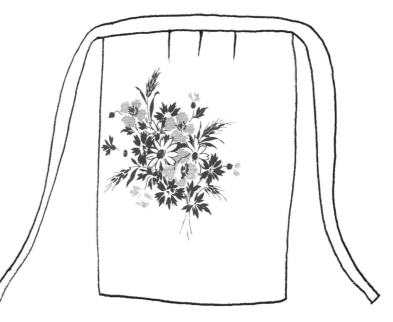

let the housewifey chores begin... or simply don a pair of fluffy mules to accessorize your apron and kick back with a well-deserved drink!

shopping bag.

things you need

1 piece of medium or heavyweight cotton canvas, approximately 21in x 38in (54cm x 96cm).

2 pieces of medium or heavyweight cotton canvas for the handles, approximately 24in x 4¾in (60cm x 12cm).

apples, pears, milk, eggs, and french bread always look better in a chic floral or striped cotton shopping bag. this shopper is easy to make and is a wonderful way to recycle old curtains—not to mention helping the cause by cutting down on the plastic carrier. super strong for lots of shopping, this bag is neat enough to fold up and pop in your purse.

make the handles.

for each handle fold a ⅜in (1cm) hem over to the wrong side along all four edges of the fabric piece and press. then fold the fabric in half lengthwise so the turned edges meet. press and pin. stitch together all the way around, stitching as close to the edge as possible for a neat finish. backstitch at the start and finish to fasten the seam.

⅜in (1cm)

make the bag.

fold the main body in half crosswise with right sides together. pin in place. stitch both sides and the bottom together with a ⅜in (1cm) seam. trim the three seam edges with pinking shears.

hem the bag.

fold a ⅜in (1cm) hem over to the wrong side along the top edge of the bag and press (it helps to use the end of the ironing board to do this). repeat this for a second time so the raw edge of the fabric is concealed. pin in place then stitch all the way around the top edge, stitching as close to the inside edge of the hem as possible. backstitch at the start and finish to fasten the seam.

make the base and sides.

flatten out the bag so that the two side edges are lined up in the center. open out the bottom edge into a square. mark a triangle at the top and bottom corners of this square as follows. from the point of the triangle measure 2¼in (6cm) in along each edge and mark with tailor's chalk. draw a line across to join these two marked points together. stitch across the chalk line. backstitch at the start and finish to fasten the seam. it is a good idea to stitch these seams twice for double strength. trim the excess corner fabric with pinking shears. repeat for the second corner. this makes a 4in (10cm) wide base/side section. turn the bag right side out.

2¼in (6cm)

attach the handles.

on the right side of the bag position one end of a handle 4in (10cm) in from the side seam and 2¼in (6cm) down from the top edge. position the other end of the handle to match at the opposite side. pin in place. stitch the handle to the bag; for extra strength stitch a rectangle and then add a cross in the middle. repeat on the other side of the bag with the second handle.

fold up and place in your purse ready for any impromptu shopping trips!

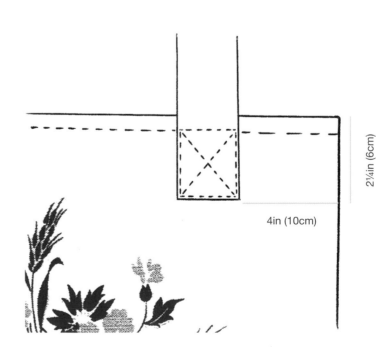

2¼in (6cm)

4in (10cm)

for the living room

café curtain.

things you need

1 piece of lightweight cotton fabric for curtain panel, at least ¾in (2cm) larger all around than the size of your window.

lightweight cotton fabric for the loops, 1½in x 4¾in (4cm x 12cm) per loop—you will need one loop for every 4in (10cm) of curtain width.

wooden dowel.

flat latex paint and paintbrush (a tester pot should do the trick).

2 screw hooks and screw eyes.

inspired by the classic café curtain, this simple and attractive window treatment is ideal for covering the lower half of any window (although preferably one with a wooden frame). it affords privacy without blocking out all the light, and is a great way to add color and pattern to a room at the same time.

measure.
to determine the size of the curtain panel required, measure your window and add 1½in (4cm) to both the height and the width to give a ¾in (2cm) hem allowance on each side. cut the panel piece to size.

make the loops.
fold a ⅜in (1cm) hem over to the wrong side along all four sides of each fabric piece and press. then fold the fabric in half lengthwise so the two folded edges meet. press and pin. stitch all the way around the loop, stitching as close to the edge as possible for a neat finish. backstitch at the start and finish to fasten the seam. repeat this for all loops.

⅜in (1cm)

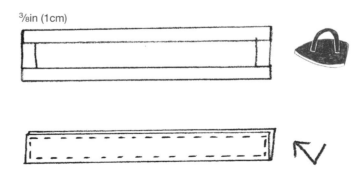

hem the curtain panel.

fold a ⅜in (1cm) hem over to the wrong side along each edge of the fabric piece and press. repeat this all the way around for a second time so the raw edge of the fabric is concealed. take care not to pull the fabric out of shape and to make neat corners as you press. pin in place then stitch all the way around, stitching as close to the inside edge of the hem as possible. backstitch at the start and finish to fasten the seam.

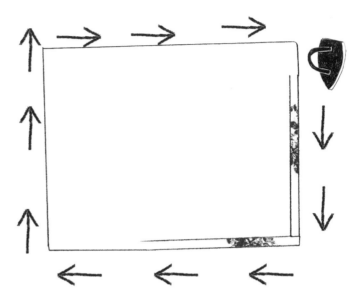

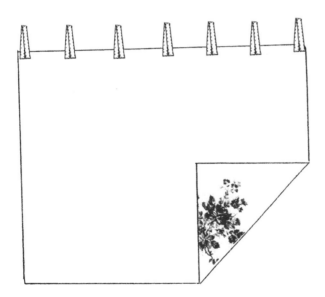

attach the loops.

fold each of the loops in half crosswise and press. starting at the outer edges of the curtain panel and working in toward the center, position the loops on the wrong side of the panel at the top edge at regular intervals of 4in (10cm) or thereabouts. to make attaching the loops easier, lay the two ends of each loop side by side rather than one end on top of the other (this makes the curtain less bulky and easier to stitch). pin each loop in place. stitch the loops to the curtain panel, stitching ¼in (5mm) in from the top edge. backstitch each loop a couple of times to fasten securely. press.

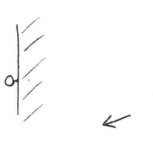

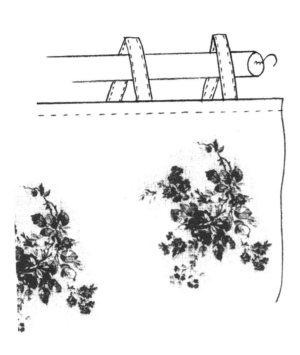

hang the curtain.

cut the wooden dowel to the width
of the window frame, allowing
a small gap for the hooks and
eyes—⅜in (1cm) at either end
should do the trick. paint the
dowel the color of your choice—
i used a regular white latex. once
the paint is dry, screw the hooks
into both ends of the dowel and
affix the screw eyes in place on
the window frame. pass the dowel
through all the loops, then hook
the complete curtain and dowel
in place on the hooks. there you
have it!

seat cushion.

things you need

1 large sheet of paper or newspaper.

medium weight cotton or linen for the main cushion—around 20in x 40in (50cm x 100cm) per cushion should do it.

2 pieces of medium weight cotton for the ties, 1½in x 16in (4cm x 40cm).

foam or batting for the filling—20in x 20in x 1½in (50cm x 50cm x 4cm) thick should be plenty, but check against your seat pattern to be sure you have enough.

1 upholstery zipper (to match the width of the back of your chair seat—see applying a zipper on pages 22–3).

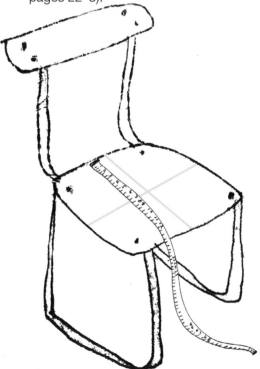

wooden kitchen chairs—available in a wondrous collection of shapes and sizes—are rather lovely in my eyes, but after a lengthy sunday lunch or a five-course dinner they can become a touch uncomfortable for the derrière. to maximize comfort, add a nice soft cushion. seat cushions are relatively easy to make and, with ties at the back to hold them in place, they are the perfect accompaniment to a long-lasting lunch.

measure.

measure the depth and width of the chair seat; a seat is often wider at the front than the back and this needs to be taken into account when drawing out the pattern. for the seat pieces draw the exact shape of the chair seat onto the paper and then add a ⅜in (1cm) seam allowance all the way around. you will also need patterns for the side panels, front panel, and back panel. the side panels are the same length as the sides of the seat pieces, and 2¼in (6cm) deep. similarly, the front panel is the same width as the front of the seat piece, 2¼in (6cm) deep, and the back panel is as wide as the back of the seat piece, and 2¼in (6cm) deep.

cut out the pieces.

cut your fabric pieces using the patterns. you will need two main seat pieces, two side panels, one front panel, and one back panel.

make the ties.

fold a ⅜in (1cm) hem over to the wrong side along all four sides of each fabric piece and press. then fold the fabric in half lengthwise so the two folded edges meet. press and pin. stitch all the way around the tie, stitching as close to the edge as possible for a neat finish. backstitch at the start and finish to fasten the seam. repeat this for all ties.

apply the zipper.

apply the zipper to the back panel as follows: cut the panel in half lengthwise and fold a ⅜in (1cm) hem over to the wrong side along the length of one side on each piece. press and pin. then follow the instructions for applying a zipper as given on pages 22–3.

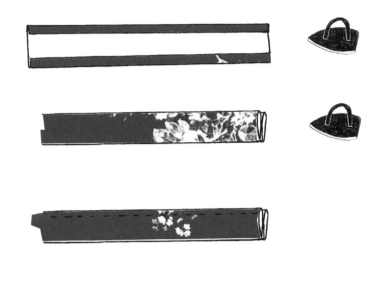

make the boxing strip.

close the zipper applied to the back panel. with right sides together, pin one end of each side panel to the ends of the back panel with raw edges even. stitch a ⅜in (1cm) seam. backstitch at the start and finish to fasten the seam. press the seams open. repeat this to join the front panel to the other ends of the side panels, pressing the seams open once sewn. you should end up with a floppy rectangle shape, which is the cushion boxing strip.

join the seat pieces.

with right sides together pin the boxing strip to the bottom seat piece. i find it easier to start with the back and work my way around, pinning as i go and making sure the seams meet as planned in the corners. follow the instructions for sewing box corners as given on page 18. stitch the boxing strip in place with one continuous ⅜in (1cm) seam. backstitch at the start and finish to fasten the seam. (make sure the zipper is open for the next part as you will need to get a hand in to turn the cushion cover right side out once you have finished stitching.) repeat this process to join the boxing strip to the top seat piece. turn the cover right side out and press the seams (the edge of the ironing board helps with this).

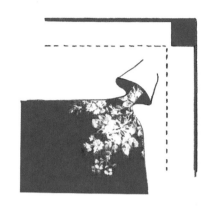

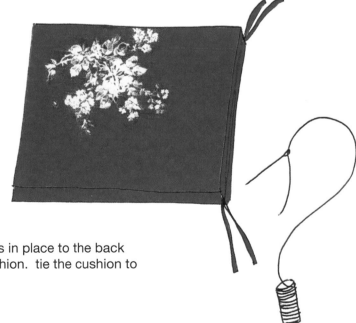

add the padding.

using the seat pattern, cut the foam or batting to the correct size to fit your cushion cover. you will need to use a sharp craft knife and take extra care when cutting. stuff the cushion cover with the cut foam or batting.

add the ties.

hand stitch the ties in place to the back corners of the cushion. tie the cushion to the chair.

roman shade.

things you need

1 piece of main fabric, the size of the window to be covered plus 2in (5cm) in width and plus 6in (15cm) in length for the header and hem.

1 piece of lining fabric, the size of the window to be covered plus 2in (5cm) in width and plus 6in (15cm) in length for the header and hem.

bias binding, 1in (2.5cm) wide, ¾in (2cm) longer than the width of the shade.

1 wooden dowel, ⅜in (9mm) in diameter, the width of the shade less ¾in (2cm).

binding tape, calculated by the number of rows and the height of the shade: you need one vertical row every 12in (30cm) across the width of the shade.

metal rings, calculated by the number of rows and the height of the shade: on each row you need a ring every 6in (15cm) across the width of the shade).

1 wooden header board (sanded and smoothed) the width of the window by 1in (2.5cm) and 2in (5cm).

large screw eyes (quantity to match number of rows of tape).

strong cord (double the height of each row plus the distance from the top of each row across to the side of the shade).

1 cleat for the window

upholstery tacks and hammer

brackets and screws to fit the header board above the frame

wooden beads (optional)

fantastically neat and relatively easy to make (with a bit of patience), the roman shade is my first port of call when a window needs dressing. a medium-weight cotton drill or indian dupion silk works well for this shade.

measure.
to determine the size of the shade panel required, measure your window and add 2in (5cm) to the width and 6in (15cm) to the height. cut the main piece and lining fabric to size, being sure to cut as straight as possible.

seam the main panel.
place the main panel and lining pieces with right sides together. pin around three sides leaving the top open. stitch a ⅜in (1cm) seam. backstitch at the start and finish to fasten the seam. clip the corners (see pages 18–9), then turn the main panel right side out. push the seam and corners out fully, pressing as you go.

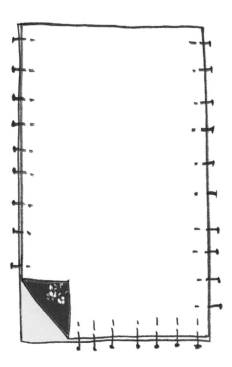

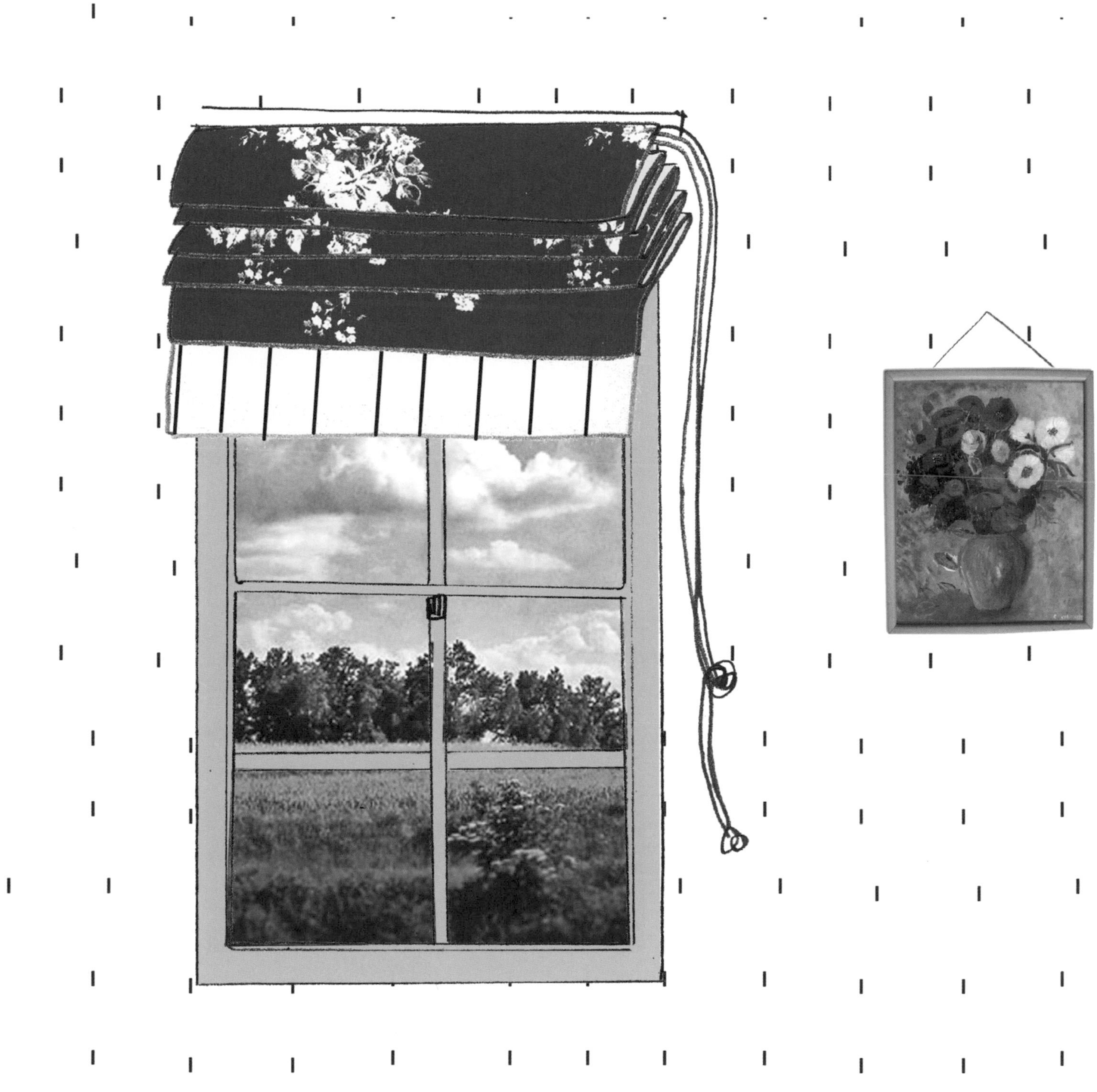

bind the main panel.

pin the bias binding along the top edge of the main panel. turn the raw edge of the binding under by ⅜in (1cm) at the ends to give a neat finish. stitch this in place all the way along, taking care to catch the bias binding on both sides as you sew. backstitch at the start and finish to fasten the seam.

mark up the dowel casing.

lay the shade out flat with the lining side up. using a yardstick or straight edge and tailor's chalk or soft pencil, measure 5½in (14cm) from the bottom and draw a horizontal line across the shade. draw a second line just above the first to mark the casing for the dowel. the casing must fit the dowel rod snugly rather than be too loose: ½in (12mm) should be fine to fit a ⅜in (9mm) diameter dowel but this may vary slightly depending on the weight of the fabric.

add the tape.

position the strips of tape vertically on the shade, working from the upper casing line to the top edge. starting at the outer edges of the panel and working in toward the center, position the strips of tape ⅜in (1cm) in from the outer edges and then at equal intervals of 12in (30cm) or thereabouts. when you are happy with the position of each strip, mark these lines on the shade with the yardstick and tailor's chalk. pin or baste each of the strips in place, tucking the ends under to conceal the raw edges as you go. stitch each strip in place. start each line of stitching from the top so the fabric does not pucker. backstitch at the start and finish to fasten the seam. slipstitch by hand the ends of each strip of tape to finish.

stitch the dowel casing.

stitch the two horizontal casing lines. backstitch at the start and finish to fasten the seams.

attach the rings.

position the metal rings along each strip of tape, 6in (15cm) apart, making sure that the rings form exactly level horizontal lines across the shade. securely hand stitch the rings in place.

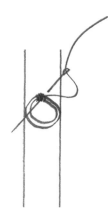

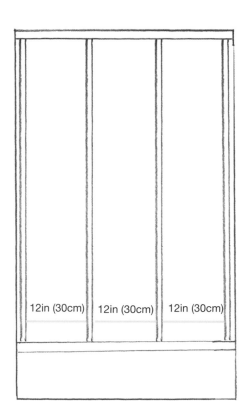

12in (30cm)   12in (30cm)   12in (30cm)

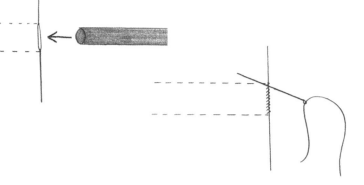

add the dowel.

unpick the side seam along one edge of the dowel casing to make an opening. slot the dowel in place. slipstitch by hand to reseal the opening.

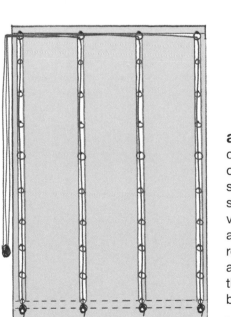

attach the shade to the header board.

position the top 6in (15mm) of the shade, lining side down, over the edge of the header board. hammer tacks all the way across the top edge to secure in place.

add the screw eyes.

affix the screw eyes to the underside of the header board directly level with the rows of metal rings on the back of the shade.

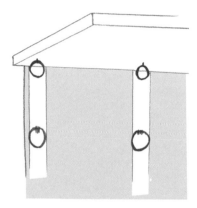

add the cord.

cut a length of cord for each individual row of metal rings on the shade: each cord must be double the height of the shade plus the distance from the row of rings to the side—so each cord will vary in length as the distance to the side varies. thread each cord through its row of rings and across all the screw eyes. knot each cord to the bottom ring of its row. knot the cords together just beyond the last screw eye and again at their ends to keep them tidy. trim the cords to the same length and attach the wooden beads (not essential but a nice touch).

hang the shade.

mount the brackets and the header board above the window frame. at a comfortable height attach the cleat to the side of the window frame (or the wall if this is easier) for securing the cord when the shade is pulled up. to set the pleats in the shade, keep in the pulled-up position for the first few days.

bolster.

things you need

1 piece of medium weight cotton or linen, 25¼in x 19¼in (64cm x 49cm), if you are hand stitching the zipper. *or* 2 pieces of medium weight cotton or linen, each 13in x 18in (33cm x 46cm), if you are machine stitching the zipper.

2 disks of cotton or linen, 8¼in (21cm) in diameter.

2 buttons (mismatched vintage ones are good for this).

1 upholstery zipper, 18in (46cm) long.

1 feather-filled bolster, 18in (46cm) long by 8in (20cm) in diameter.

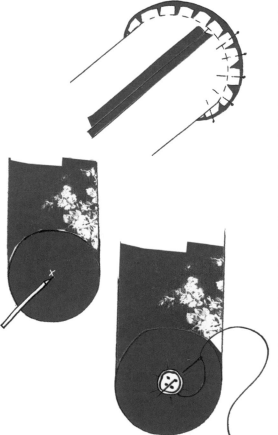

traditionally used on the bed, the bolster is great for plumping up when reading and snuggling up to when sleeping. as well as providing extra support, for me they are equally fabulous for dressing up a sofa, armchair, daybed, or chaise lounge!

apply the zipper.
when using a sewing machine, applying a zipper is much easier with two panels of fabric. i used two panels of contrasting fabric for the bolster pictured opposite. to fit the zipper between two panels of fabric, fold a ⅜in (1cm) hem over to the wrong side along the length of one side on each piece. press and pin. then follow the instructions for applying a zipper as given on pages 22–3. if you choose to use a single panel of fabric the technique is the same; however, i recommend fitting the zipper by hand as keeping the excess fabric out of the way of the sewing machine needle is particularly tricky.

join the main panels.
if using two panels you will need to join them. with right sides together, place the long edges of the panels together so the raw edges are even. pin and stitch a ⅜in (1cm) seam. backstitch at the start and finish to fasten the seam. press the seams open.

fit the end panels.
prepare the main piece for fitting the end panels by making a round of ⅜in (1cm) cuts, ¾in (2cm) apart, at each end. with the zipper half open, pin the end disks in place. stitch a ⅝in (1.5cm) seam. this is a little tricky so take your time: if you need to add a little pleat here and there to make it fit, then do.

attach the buttons.
turn the bolster cover right side out. with tailor's chalk, mark the center point at each end. hand stitch the buttons in place, gathering the fabric in slightly to create a puckered effect. finish with a double knot and wind the excess thread around the button.

add the bolster.
stuff the cover with the feather bolster and close the zipper.

patched pillow.

things you need

4 pieces of lightweight linen or medium weight cotton damask or linen in the following sizes:

1 large front panel, 20½in x 11in (52cm x 28cm).

1 medium front panel, 20½ in x 6¼in (52cm x 16cm).

1 small front panel, 20½in x 4¾in (52cm x 12cm).

1 back panel, 20½in x 20½in (52cm x 52cm).

1 upholstery zipper, 20in (50cm) long.

1 piece of cotton fabric for zipper end, ⅜in x 1¼in (1cm x 3cm).

1 feather-filled pillow form, 20in x 20in (50cm x 50cm).

pillows are a fantastic yet simple way to update any room large enough to house a chair or sofa. they can be easily made in a variety of shapes, sizes, and fabric combinations.

if you are using patterned or vintage fabric, keep to a particular color scheme for an elegant, eclectic look. or, for a bolder look, really mix things up with complementary colors, patterns, and shapes for a bright and modern statement.

in this instance i have teamed my favorite linen of the moment—a deep petrol blue with a floral print—with a plain oatmeal linen and a panel of vintage cotton damask.

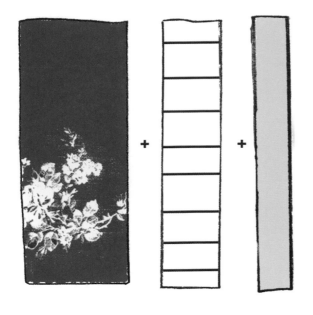

join the panels.
with right sides together, pin the small panel to the medium panel along one long edge and stitch a ⅜in (1cm) seam. backstitch at the start and finish to fasten the seam. place the large panel and unstitched side of the medium panel together, with right sides together. pin and stitch a ⅜in (1cm) seam. press the two seams open.

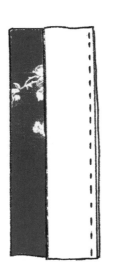

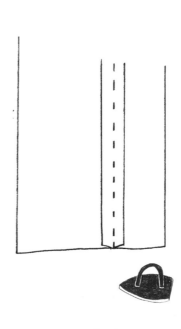

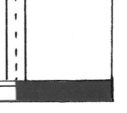

hem the panels.
fold a ⅜in (1cm) hem over to the wrong side along the bottom edge of the front panel and press. repeat this for the back panel.

apply the zipper.

attach the zipper end to the zipper as given on page 22. unzip the zipper to over halfway. (this is so you will be able to get a hand in to turn the cover right side out once you have finished stitching. i have forgotten to do this on many occasions; it is very annoying as you have to unpick and start again!) follow the instructions for applying a zipper as given on pages 22–3, placing the two panels right sides together, making sure they are lined up with the zipper edge. if the top of the pillow is slightly out do not worry—the essential thing is that the zipper edge is lined up. use the zipper edge as your straight line to work from to make a neatly stitched square.

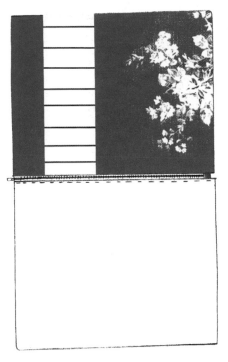

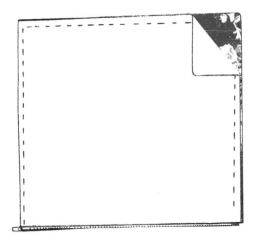

join the front and back.

pin the panels in place. starting from the "zipper end" corner, stitch the three edges of the pillow cover together with a ⅜in (1cm) seam. trim the raw edges of the seams with pinking shears to finish them.

add the pillow form.

turn the pillow cover right side out and press. stuff with the pillow form, *et voilà!*

antimacassar.

things you need

1 piece of lightweight cotton, 14in x 17in (36cm x 42cm) or thereabouts.

2 buttons (optional).

during victorian times it was very fashionable for the gentlemen to groom their hair with a concoction of palm and coconut oils, named macassar oil. this pomade was not overly popular with the housewives of the time as it had a tendency to soil the permanent fabric on the head of the armchair or sofa. to overcome this problem, these inventive ladies covered the back and arms of seats with a fabric cloth that could be removed periodically to be cleaned... and so the antimacassar was born.

the addition of a couple of buttons, hand stitched to the back of the chair, is an excellent way to hold the antimacassar in place.

hem the panel.

fold a ⅜in (1cm) hem over to the wrong side along each edge of the fabric piece and press. repeat this all the way around for a second time so the raw edge of the fabric is concealed, taking care not to pull the fabric out of shape and to make neat corners as you press. pin in place then stitch all the way around, stitching as close to the inside edge of the hem as possible. backstitch at the start and finish to fasten the seam.

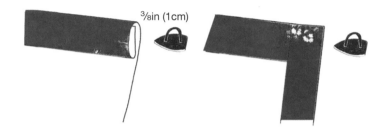

⅜in (1cm)

stitch the buttonholes.

add two buttonholes to the top edge of the antimacassar, one in each corner. to hold the antimacassar in place, hand stitch the buttons to the back of the armchair so that they match up with the buttonholes.

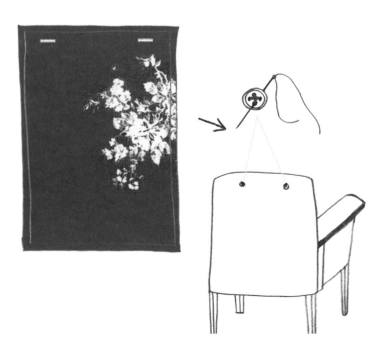

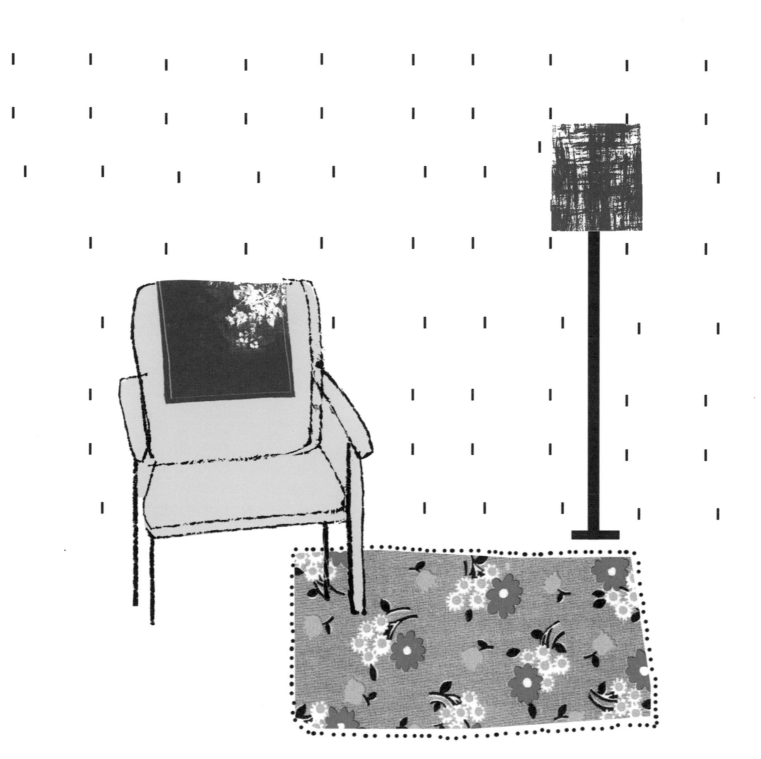

draft excluder.

things you need

2 pieces of light or medium weight petrol blue linen, the first 16½in x 16½in (42cm x 42cm) and the second 10¼in x 9½in (26cm x 24cm).

1 piece of light or medium weight oatmeal linen, 22in x 16½in (56cm x 42cm).

1 piece of medium weight cotton for the mouth, approximately 9½in x 9½in (24cm x 24cm).

2 buttons.

a little scrap of linen for his fork-shaped tongue.

stuffing (i have used old scraps of fabric as stuffing; as well as being a great bit of recycling, it makes the snake nice and weighty so that sebastian stays put).

if, like me, you suffer from drafty doors then sebastian the draft excluder is the chap for you! he doubles up as a guard snake at the same time, so watch out for ankle nipping when you walk past. this is a really easy project to make; the beauty of this design is that it only takes a little tweak here and there— a change of color, a longer tongue, a different eye position—to create a whole new personality for the snake.

join the panels.

with right sides together, pin the short edge of the oatmeal panel to the larger blue panel and stitch a ⅜in (1cm) seam. backstitch at the start and finish to fasten the seam. pin the remaining blue panel to the unstitched side of the oatmeal panel with right sides together. pin and stitch a ⅜in (1cm) seam. press the two seams open.

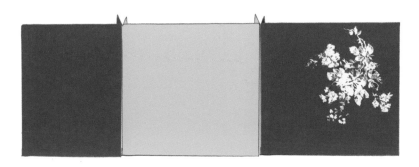

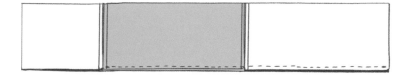

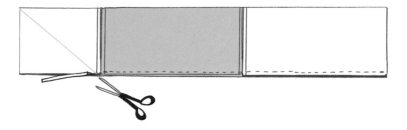

make the body.
with right sides together, fold the fabric in half lengthwise. pin and stitch the long edges, starting at the end of the larger blue panel but stitching only up to the end of the oatmeal panel, leaving the smaller blue panel unstitched. backstitch at the start and finish to fasten the seam.

make the tail.
lay the body out flat with the long seamed edge closest to you. using a straight edge and tailor's chalk, draw a line across the smaller blue panel from the bottom right corner (at the seam line where it joins the oatmeal panel) to the top left-hand corner. cut through both layers of fabric $\frac{3}{8}$in (1cm) below this line, removing the bottom triangle shape you have just marked out. this will form the tail.

make the head.
lay the body out flat again, this time with the long seam running down the center of the body. on the larger blue panel (head end) mark a point on the top edge, 4¾in (12cm) in from the corner. mark another point 4¾in (12cm) in from the bottom corner. draw two lines to join these points to the center of the side edge, at the end of the seam. cut through both layers of fabric, $\frac{3}{8}$in (1cm) outside these lines, removing the two outer triangle shapes you have just marked out. this will form the head.

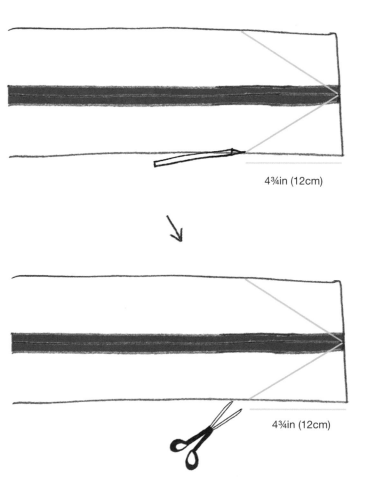

4¾in (12cm)

4¾in (12cm)

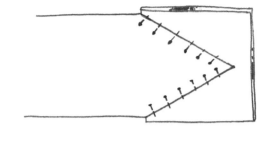

make the mouth.

with the right side facing inward, fold the fabric piece for the mouth in half. slot this folded panel into the point you have just cut on the head piece; the folded edge must butt right up to the two corner points of the main head piece. working along one side at a time, pin the top layer of the pointed head piece to the top layer of the mouth panel. turn over and repeat on the other side. now stitch all the way around the mouth, following the line of the point, with a ⅜in (1cm) seam. backstitch at the start and finish to fasten the stitch. this can be a little tricky, but if you lay the mouth panel flat so the point is open as far as it can go, it just takes a little time and patience. start at the point on the one side and work your way around, taking care at the corners of the mouth. if a little pleat is required here and there, that's fine. it will simply add to the snake's personality. trim any excess fabric from the mouth panel with pinking shears (any waste can be used for stuffing).

stuff the snake.

turn the snake right side out, making sure all corners and crevices are fully turned out. your work should now resemble a floppy snakelike character. stuff the snake, starting at the mouth and working down to the tail. when you get to the pointed tail end, have a needle and thread at the ready. continue to stuff and stitch as you go, tucking the raw edges under and using blanket stitch (see page 15) to close the seam.

add the finishing touches.

once your snake is fully stuffed and the tail end stitched up, you are ready to add its eyes and tongue to bring him to life! i securely stitched two buttons on the top of sebastian's head as a pair of eyes. then i cut a fork-shaped snake's tongue from a scrap of the oatmeal linen, which i hand stitched to the middle of his mouth.

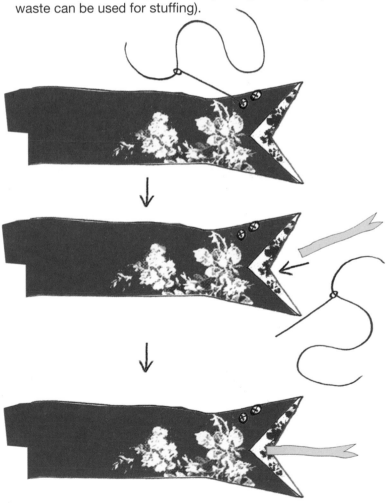

ottoman.

things you need

for the lining:

1 piece of heavyweight muslin, 17in x 58in (43cm x 147cm).

3 disks of heavyweight muslin, 18in (46cm) in diameter.

16½in (42cm) length of sew-in velcro, ¾in (2cm) wide.

for the outer body:

1 piece of cotton drill, denim, or similar weight fabric, 17in x 58in (43cm x 147cm).

3 disks of cotton drill, denim, or similar weight fabric, 18in (46cm) in diameter.

60in (150cm) of piping.

double-ended upholstery needle.

4 buttons.

stuffing (either scraps of fabric or wood shavings).

there is nothing more relaxing than sitting in a comfortable armchair with your feet up on an ottoman, which also works very well as emergency seating if your living room is overflowing with guests. when making them at home, stuffing with scraps of fabric creates a firm and weighty ottoman while putting all those waste bits and pieces to good use. wood shavings work equally well.

make the lining.

take one of the muslin disks and measure 11in (28cm) across the diameter. mark a straight line across the circle at this point and cut along the line. repeat for the second disk. fold a ⅜in (1cm) hem over to the wrong side along the straight edges of the part circle and press. repeat this for a second time so the raw edge of the fabric is concealed. pin and then stitch. backstitch at the start and finish to fasten the seam. repeat for the second part circle.

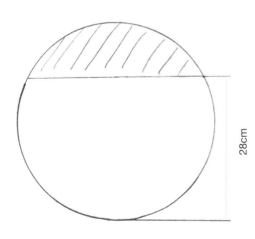

28cm

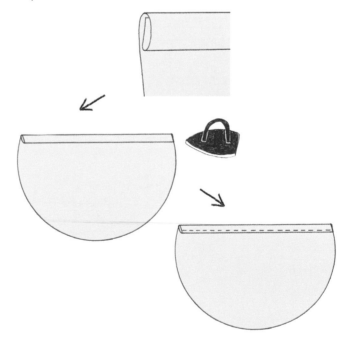

add the velcro.

these two part circles overlap to make a full circle; the velcro is fitted to the overlap to create a fastening that keeps the stuffing in place. separate the velcro. on the wrong side of the first part circle, place one half of the velcro strip along the straight edge. pin and stitch. place the second part circle over the first part circle and overlap them so that they create a full circle. place the second half of the velcro strip across the right side of the second part circle so that it lines up with the first velcro strip. pin and stitch. fasten the two velcro edges together to complete the circle. set to one side.

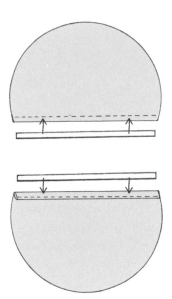

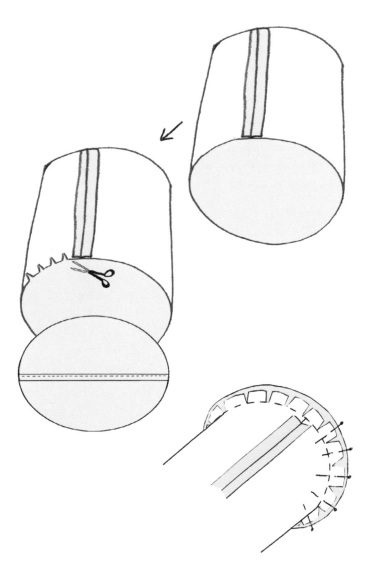

join the side seam.

with right sides together, place the two short edges of the rectangular lining piece together to create a tube. pin and stitch with a ⅝in (1.5cm) seam. backstitch at the start and finish to fasten the seam. (it is worth double stitching this seam for extra strength.) press the seam open.

fit the end panels.

prepare the main lining piece for fitting the end disks by making a round of ⅜in (1cm) cuts, ¾in (2cm) apart, at each end. pin the end disks in place. stitch a ⅝in (1.5cm) seam. (again, it is worth taking the time to double stitch these seams for extra strength.)

prepare the cover.

cut and hem two of the outer fabric disks in the same way as the lining. baste together to make a complete circle. position and baste the piping all the way around the edge of the remaining outer fabric circle, matching the raw edges and finishing the ends (see page 21).

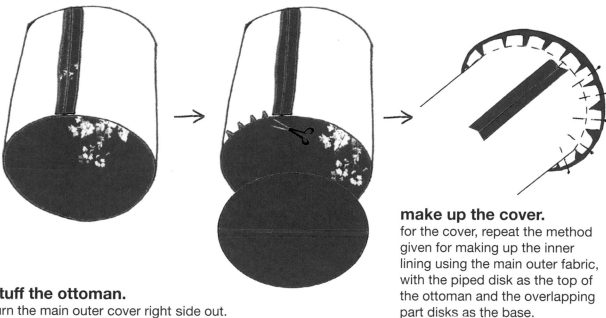

make up the cover.

for the cover, repeat the method given for making up the inner lining using the main outer fabric, with the piped disk as the top of the ottoman and the overlapping part disks as the base.

stuff the ottoman.

turn the main outer cover right side out. insert the inner lining to fit snugly inside with the base openings lined up. fill the ottoman with your chosen stuffing—either fabric scraps or wood shavings—until it is firm. fasten the velcro in the lining and overlap the outer fabric cover.

add the buttons.

a very nice decorative touch is to add four buttons to the top of the ottoman. with tailor's chalk, mark four equally spaced points on the top of the ottoman. using a double-ended long upholstery needle, attach the four buttons, gathering the fabric up slightly as you sew.

now put your feet up and have a steaming hot cup of coffee.

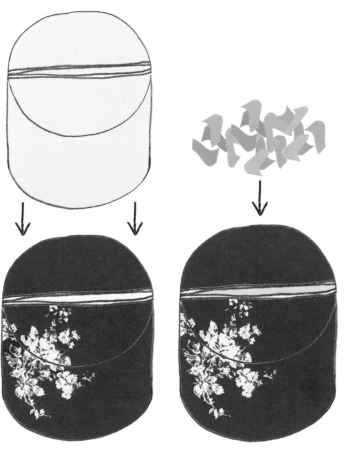

winter curtain.

things you need

- curtain fabric (i recommend heavyweight linen or tasar silk), see "measure" for quantity.
- curtain lining fabric (preferably in cream or white), see "measure" for quantity.
- 3in (7.5cm) self-styling header tape.
- brass curtain hooks.
- curtain pole.
- curtain rings (i used painted wooden ones).
- a large, clear space to work and plenty of cups of coffee!

curtains can be fantastical and theatrical; the detail and work that goes into most, from the fabric to their construction, can result in a stunning window treatment. complicated, fussy components, such as cornices, ruffles, weights, and other fancy bits, confuse the issue and often scare off the home sewer. however, this winter curtain employs the simplest curtain-making methods i have found and so is designed to be a relatively straightforward make.

for the instructions, i have tried my best to explain every stage in the most direct way possible. the idea is for you to be able to make a functional yet elegant curtain for your home without throwing your sewing machine out of the window in anger. although these curtains are particularly splendid in scale, they are hopefully not too scary to attempt.

the success of this curtain design lies in the fabric you choose to make it in. matching up repeat patterns on a curtain of this grand a scale is where things start to get really tricky, so if it is your first attempt at sewing curtains, i would take the easiest route. i recommend using a beautifully plain but weighty fabric, such as a tasar silk, and perhaps adding in a panel of a contrasting fabric to add interest.

measure.

for the main fabric

a pair of curtains or a single curtain?
more often than not, you will need a pair of
curtains for a window. however, if your window is
20in (50cm) wide or less, a single curtain will be much
more suitable, which can be swept to one side and
secured with a complementary tieback.

width of the curtain
as this is a fairly heavy winter curtain, fit the pole 5in
(12cm) above the window frame and so that it extends
5in (12cm) either side. to achieve a well-fitted curtain,
measure the width of the curtain pole and not the
window. when using a self-styling header tape, as in this
case, the width of each curtain in the pair needs to be
approximately two and a half times the curtain pole plus
a ⅜in (1cm) seam allowance on each side of the width.
check the amount of fullness recommended by the tape
manufacturer. (for the curtain pictured, i used three
panels of fabric per curtain that were stitched together to
obtain the required size.)

length of the curtain
i have taken the length of each curtain right to the floor
so they puddle in a contemporary fashion. this has two
benefits: the first is that it looks stylishly modern and
the second (more important) is that it eliminates any
possibility of incorrect measuring resulting in curtains
that are too short! after measuring from the pole to the
floor, add an additional 10in (25cm) to the length for the
curtain's "puddle" and hem.

for the lining fabric
this needs to be 7in (18cm) shorter than the main fabric,
and 2¼in (6cm) less on the width.

for the self-styling header tape
this needs to match the width of the main fabric.

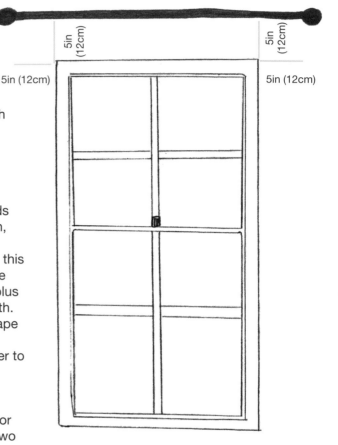

5in (12cm)

5in (12cm)

5in (12cm)

5in (12cm)

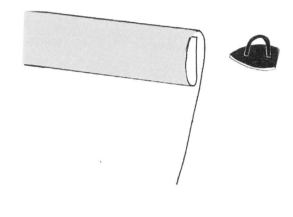

make the curtain panel.

fold a ⅜in (1cm) hem over to the wrong side along the bottom edge of a lining piece and press. repeat to conceal the raw edge. press and pin. stitch the hem. backstitch at the start and finish to fasten the seam. right sides together, pin the lining to the main fabric with the top edges even. on one side stitch a ⅜in (1cm) seam from top to bottom. backstitch at the start and finish to fasten the seam. repeat this on the opposite side to make an enormous tube. press the seams open. turn the curtain panel right side out.

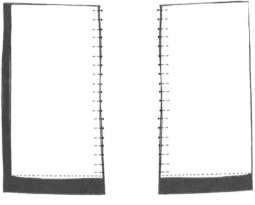

¾in (2cm)   ¾in (2cm)

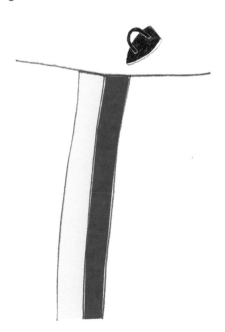

press the curtain panel.

with the lining face up, press the curtain panel flat so that the lining is centrally positioned and the excess main fabric is equally divided on either side; there should be approximately a ¾in (2cm) strip of main fabric at both sides.

3⁄8in (1cm)

hem the curtain panel.
fold a 3⁄8in (1cm) hem over to the wrong side along the top of the curtain. flatten the folded edges together, lining to main, so they form a neat straight hem. pin and hand baste the layers together (these basting stitches will be removed at a later stage).

add the header tape.
position the self-styling header tape over the lining 3⁄8in (1cm) down from the top of the curtain panel and leaving an overhang of 1in (2.5cm) at each end. pin in place along the top and bottom edges only of the header tape. if you are making a pair of curtains, at this stage you must work out which is the inner edge of your curtain (the one that will sit in the center of the window when the curtains are closed). at the inner edge, on the underside of the overhanging header tape, pull out the cords from the first three slots on both top and bottom edges using your scissors. knot these cords securely together on the wrong side. fold under the header tape so that the knot is hidden and pin in place. on the outer edge, on the top side of the overhanging header tape, pull out the cords as before. knot these cords securely together. (the cords on this side need to be accessible so you can draw them up at a later stage.) fold under the excess header tape and pin in place.

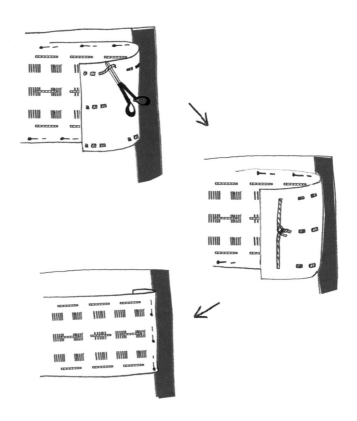

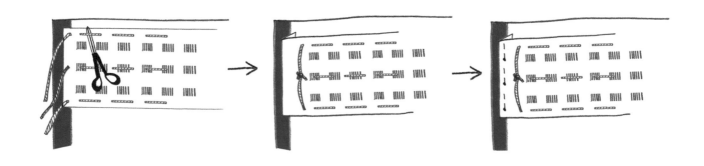

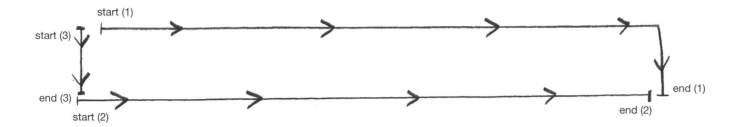

stitch the header tape.

when sewing the header tape in place, you need to keep the curtain absolutely flat and make sure you do not stitch over the cord. the best way to do this is to start at the top left-hand edge, 1in (2.5cm) in, and stitch all the way along, stitching as close to the edge as possible for a neat finish. when you reach the end, turn a 90° corner and stitch down the right-hand edge. backstitch at the start and finish to fasten the seam, then cut the thread. starting again at the left-hand edge, stitch the bottom edge of the header tape in the same direction as you stitched the top edge. backstitch at the start and finish to fasten the seam, then cut the thread. stitch the left-hand edge of the header tape securely in place to finish. remove the basting stitches from the top hem.

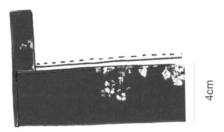

hem the curtain.

fold a ⅜in (1cm) hem over to the wrong side along the bottom edge of the curtain. fold a further 1½in (4cm) hem over so the raw edge of the fabric is concealed and press. pin in place and stitch the hem. backstitch at the start and finish to fasten.

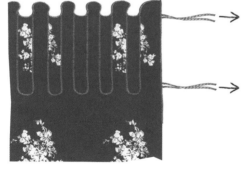

gather the curtain.

to form the pleats simply pull the preknotted cords on the header tape until the curtain reaches the desired width. (this should be slightly wider than half the width of the curtain pole, so the pair of curtains meet in the middle when closed.) adjust the pleats so they are neat and uniform. two pairs of hands are useful at this stage, especially if your curtains are on the large side. do not cut off the cord you have pulled up.

fit the hooks.

place the hooks at regular intervals along the header tape. attach the hooks to the prepared curtain rings sitting on your curtain pole.

do it all again.

if you are making a pair, repeat these instructions for the second curtain.

outdoor cushion.

things you need

2 pieces of medium weight linen for the top and bottom panels, 19in x 24in (48cm x 62cm).

2 pieces of medium weight linen for the side panels, 19in x 2¾in (48cm x 7cm).

2 pieces of medium weight linen for the front and back panels, 24½in x 2¾in (62cm x 7cm).

1 upholstery zipper, 18in (46cm) long.

4¾yd (430cm) of contrast piping (optional).

8 buttons—¾in (2cm) in diameter are ideal.

double-ended upholstery needle.

strong hand-sewing thread.

1 feather-filled box cushion, 18in x 24in x 2in (46cm x 60cm x 5cm).

whether for a garden bench, patio picnic, or pebbly beach, this outdoor cushion is fantastic for lounging around in the summertime. and when it's raining outside, it is rather handy for indoors too!

apply the zipper.

apply the zipper to one of the side panels as follows: cut the panel in half lengthwise and fold a ⅜in (1cm) hem over to the wrong side along the length of one side on each piece. press and pin. then follow the instructions for applying a zipper as given on pages 22–3.

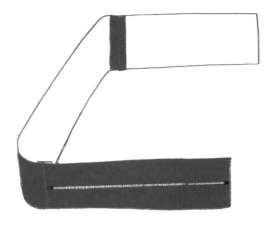
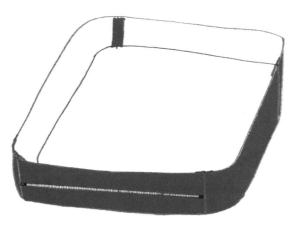

make the boxing strip.

close the zipper fitted in the side panel. with right sides together, pin one end of each side panel to the ends of the back panel so the raw edges meet. stitch a ⅜in (1cm) seam. backstitch at the start and finish to fasten the seam. press the seams open. repeat this to join the front panel to the other ends of the side panels, pressing the seams open once sewn. you should end up with a floppy rectangle shape, which is the cushion boxing strip.

add the piping.

if you are adding piping (as i have done in the cushion pictured), baste this in place all the way around the edge of the bottom and top panels. follow the instructions for adding piping as given on page 21.

join the top and bottom pieces.

with the right sides together, pin the boxing strip to the bottom panel. i find it easier to start with the zipper panel and work my way around, pinning as i go and making sure the seams meet as planned in the corners. follow the instructions for sewing box corners as given on page 18. stitch the boxing strip in place with one continuous ⅜in (1cm) seam. backstitch at the start and finish to fasten the seam. (make sure the zipper is open for the next part as you will need to get a hand in to turn the cushion cover right side out once you have finished stitching.) repeat this process to join the boxing strip to the top panel. turn the cover right side out and press the seams (the edge of the ironing board helps with this).

stuff the cushion.

fill the cover with the feather-filled cushion form, making sure it neatly fills all four corners.

add the buttons.

this next bit is rather tricky. you will need a little patience and, at times, some brute force! with tailor's chalk, mark four equally spaced points on the top of the cushion. thread your double-ended upholstery needle with about 3ft (1m) of thread. secure the thread to the first marked point with a few backstitches. push the needle right through the cushion to the underside and pull the thread through. fasten the thread up and back through the first button. push the needle back through the cushion right next to the point at which you came through previously. push the needle back through to the side you started with and pull as tight as you can so the button on the opposite side makes a neat, firm indentation. the tricky bit here is to keep the first button firmly in place while you push the thread up and back through the second button in order to make the same indentation on this side. you then have to do a bit of a patient poking trick to push the needle through the buttonholes so as to stitch the two buttons together with the cushion pad sandwiched in between, making the double dimple effect. when you have managed to stitch to and fro through both buttons four or five times, fasten the stitch with a number of small backstitches underneath the first button. secure with a knot, then trim the thread and wind any excess thread around the button. repeat this for the remaining three double dimples.

after all that, i suggest relaxing in the garden on the finished cushion with a freshly made glass of lemonade!

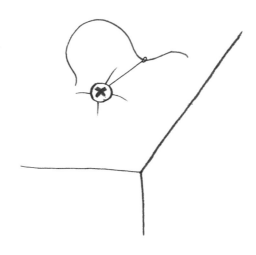

for the **bedroom**

piped pillow.

things you need

1 large sheet of paper or newspaper, at least 20in x 20in (50cm x 50cm).

pencil and a length of string.

1 piece of medium weight cotton, 20in x 40in (50cm x 100cm).

1 upholstery zipper, 19in (48cm) long.

1 feather-filled round pillow form, 18in (46cm) in diameter.

1¾yd (1.5m) of contrast piping.

a swish touch to any pillow, piping is less tricky than you may think to attach and, with a bit of practice, can take a simple pillow to a new level. i have used a complementary off-white color here, but piping can work very well indeed when highly contrasted to frame a beautiful printed fabric. i have shown both a round and a square pillow in the photograph; the two shapes are equal in terms of effort and very similar in their methods of construction.

make the template.

the best way to do this is to use the old trick of attaching a piece of string to a pencil. measure the length of string to 9½in (24cm)—half the diameter of the 19cm (48cm) circle required. with one hand, hold the end of the string in the center of the sheet of paper and with the other hand pull the string taut. draw the pencil around to create a full circle. cut out this paper pattern and then use it to cut out two circles of fabric.

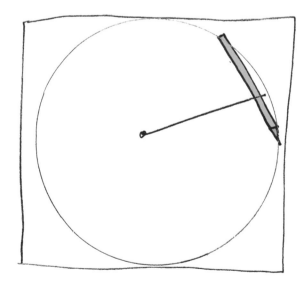

add the piping.
on the right side of the first fabric disk, pin and baste the piping in place all the way around the edge of the circle. follow the instructions for adding piping as given on page 21.

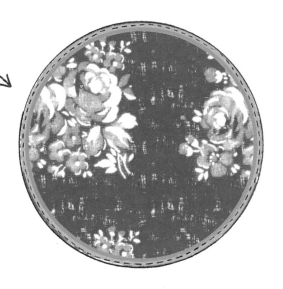

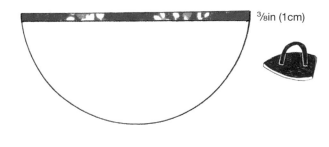

³⁄₈in (1cm)

apply the zipper.
cut the second disk in half directly down the middle. fold a ³⁄₈in (1cm) hem over to the wrong side along both straight edges. press and pin. then follow the instructions for applying a zipper as given on pages 22–3.

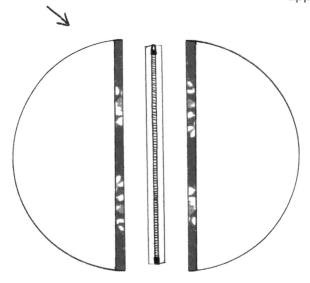

join the panels.

with right sides together, place the two prepared circles with the raw edges even. unzip the zipper to over halfway so you will be able to turn the cover right side out once stitched. with the zipper foot on the machine, pin and stitch a ½in (1cm) seam all the way around. the foot of the machine should sit just on the right-hand side of the piping so that you stitch the piping tightly and neatly in place. if you are finding it tricky, take your time and have a few practice goes on some waste fabric until you have got the hang of it. alternatively, if you have a very flashy sewing machine you may have a special piping foot, which will help no end. this is not essential, however—i always attach piping with a regular zipper foot.

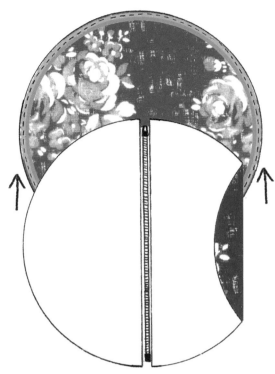

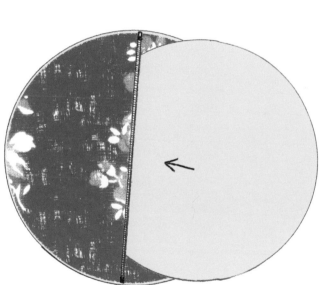

stuff the pillow.

turn the pillow cover right side out. stuff with the pillow form.

for a square pillow

this method translates fairly easily over all shapes of pillows, from square, rectangular, and even triangular if you like! it is just a little trickier on the sharper corners, but as long as you baste the piping in place first and give the corners a bit of extra time and concentration it should be trouble-free. and like everything in life, practice makes perfect!

hot-water bottle cover.

things you need

medium weight cotton (i have recycled an old soft cotton curtain) for the main body, cut to size (see template on page 142—cut 1 front piece and 2 back pieces).

4oz polyester batting, cut ¾in (2cm) smaller than the main body all the way around (see template on page 142—cut 1 front piece and 2 back pieces).

lightweight fabric (cotton muslin is ideal) for the lining, cut to size (see template on page 142—cut 1 front piece and 2 back pieces).

1¼yd (1m) of bias binding, 1in (2.5cm) wide.

nestling under the covers on a chilly winter's night with a great book, a mug of cocoa, and a hot-water bottle to toast your feet... what more could a girl want in life?

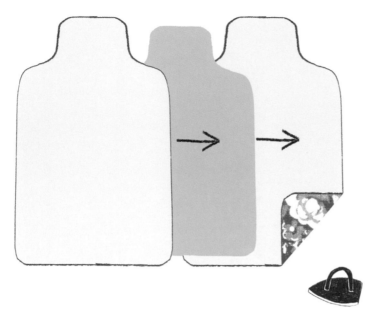

bond the panels and batting.

lay the front outer fabric piece right side down on the ironing board. lay the front batting piece on top and then the front lining piece on top of that, rather like making a sandwich. with a hot iron, press the sandwich pile so it flattens the batting slightly and loosely bonds the three layers together. repeat for the two back pieces.

add the bias binding.

cut two lengths of bias binding to slightly longer than the width of the back pieces. fold these pieces of bias binding in half lengthwise. slot one binding strip onto each of the straight edges of the back pieces. pin in place. stitch the bias binding in place, trapping all three layers neatly together. backstitch at the start and finish to fasten the seam.

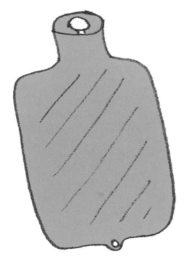

join the panels.

with right sides together, lay the top back panel on the front panel so the top edges line up. then lay the bottom back panel on top of this so the two back panels overlap in the middle and the bottom edges of the back and front panels line up. pin in place through all the layers. starting at the bottom edge, stitch all the way with a ¾in (2cm) seam. for extra strength, backstitch a couple of times when sewing over the bound edges of the top and bottom back panels. backstitch at the start and finish to fasten the seam.

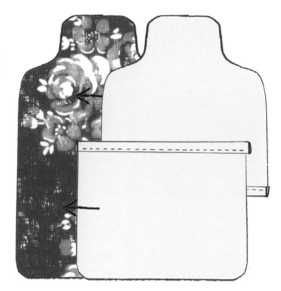

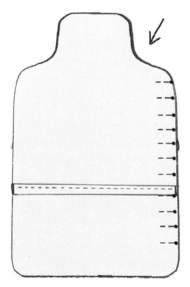

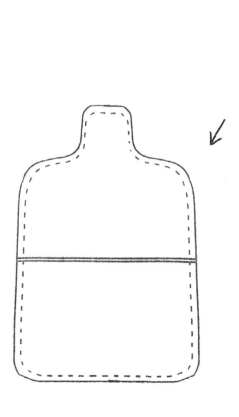

fill the cover with the hottie.

turn the hot-water bottle cover right side out, pushing out all the corners. boil the kettle, fill your hot-water bottle, and slip it into the cover.

toasty!

appliqué pillow.

things you need

2 disks of medium weight fabric (i have used linen here) for the pillow base, 20¾in (52cm) in diameter (see page 93 for drawing and cutting out).

a selection of patterned or colored fabrics for the appliqué.

1 feather-filled round pillow form, 20in (50cm) in diameter.

1 sheet of fusible web (widely available from good notions departments).

fabric crayons (optional).

1 upholstery zipper, 20in (50cm) long.

scrap cotton to use when ironing.

this project is aimed at the more artistically minded maker—let your creativity run riot and create your own fabric "collage". for the pillow shown here, i combined appliqué with a freehand drawing in fabric crayons, which offer a wonderful way to doodle on to fabric. the crayons are permanently fixed by a hot iron so they bake onto the fabric. i love the naïve quality of the drawn line combined with the intricate pattern of the vintage fabric. of course you can simply use appliqué and the lines of your stitching to create a design. even a stripe or polka dot appliqué in a patterned fabric looks very effective.

sketch your design.

this is where your own creativity comes to the fore. once you have settled on your design, the appliqué part can be as simple or as complex as you like. if you are combining appliqué with a crayon drawing this needs to be drawn and affixed to the fabric first. if you are not 100% confident drawing freehand directly onto the fabric, then practice on a sheet of paper. make sure you draw with a heavy line so the paper can be placed underneath the fabric and the drawing traced directly from it. if you are having difficulty seeing through the fabric, tape the paper drawing to a window and lay the fabric on top—the light from the window will help. trace your design with fabric crayons onto the fabric. affix the crayon drawing with a hot iron following the manufacturer's instructions.

cut out the appliqué.

when you have decided on the shape of the appliqué motifs, draw them on paper and cut out. place them face down on the paper side of the fusible web. cut out roughly, then iron onto the wrong side of the patterned fabric, following the manufacturer's instructions (these do vary slightly from brand to brand). i always lay some scrap cotton on top to protect my iron when pressing the shapes. cut the shapes out around your pencil lines and peel off the backing. position these in the desired place on your pillow front. press with a hot iron to bond together.

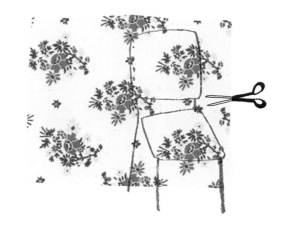

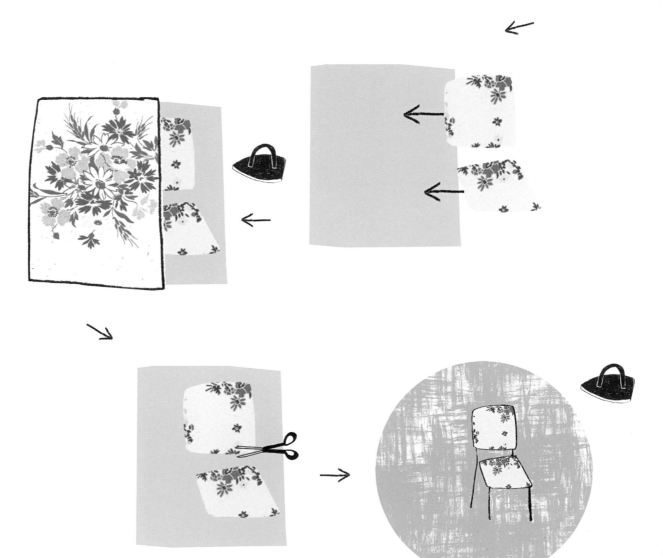

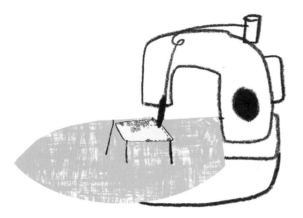

add the appliqué.
each bonded appliqué motif must be firmly stitched in place before sewing up the pillow cover. using either a contrast color thread or one matched to the color of the appliqué, carefully stitch around each shape. stitch as close to the edges as possible for a neat finish. backstitch at the start and finish to fasten.

apply the zipper.
cut the second circle in half directly down the middle. fold a ⅜in (1cm) hem over to the wrong side along both straight edges. press and pin. then follow the instructions for applying a zipper as given on pages 22–3.

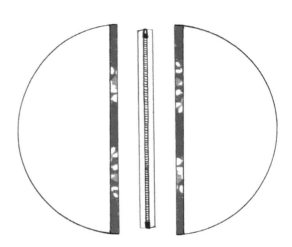

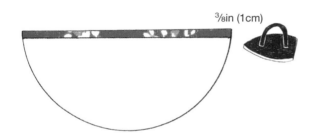

⅜in (1cm)

join the panels.
with right sides together, place the two prepared circles together so the raw edges meet. unzip the zipper to over halfway so you will be able to turn the cover right side out once stitched. pin and stitch all the way around with a ⅜in (1cm) seam. backstitch at the start and finish to secure the seam. trim the excess seam allowance with pinking shears and turn the pillow cover out to the right side and press. stuff with the feather pillow form.

done!

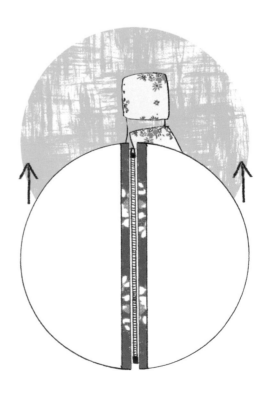

hanger coat.

things you need

2 pieces of light or medium weight cotton or silk, cut to size (see template on page 140).

1 wire coat hanger.

there is nothing more infuriating than a tangle of wire coat hangers. besides, they are not the best things in the closet to look after your favorite silk dresses. these easy-to-make but extremely functional and attractive mini coats for those troublesome wire hangers will have your closet organized and stylishly chic in no time. they are also a great way to use up odds and ends of vintage fabric!

hem the panels.

turn ¼in (5mm) over to the wrong side along the straight edge and press. repeat this for a second time so the raw edge of the fabric is concealed. pin in place. repeat this for the second panel. stitch the pressed hems, stitching as close to the inside edge of the hem as possible for a neat finish. backstitch at the start and finish to fasten the seam.

join the panels.

with right sides together, place the two pieces so the two hemmed edges are even. starting at the hemmed base, stitch a ⅜in (1cm) seam from a to b. backstitch at the start and finish to fasten the seam. then stitch a ⅜in (1cm) seam from c to d. again backstitch at the start and finish to fasten the seam.

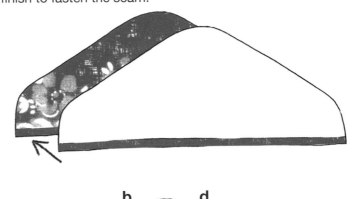

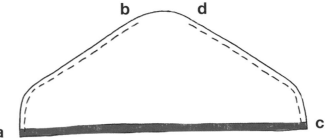

add the hanger.

turn the hanger coat right side out and press. fit the coat over the wire hanger, taking the hanger's "neck" through the hole at the top. hand stitch the hole at the top with a couple of extra stitches to secure.

suit carrier.

things you need

oilcloth fabric—60in x 60in (150cm x 150cm) will be plenty—cut to size (see template on page 141, cut 2 pieces).

1 upholstery zipper, 43in (110cm) long.

1 piece of cotton fabric for the zipper end, 1¼in x 1½in (3cm x 4cm) or thereabouts.

1 wire coat hanger (ideally with hanger coat, see page 105).

1 piece of cotton for loop, 1½in x 4in (4cm x 10cm) or thereabouts.

3½yd (3m) of bias binding, 1in (2.5cm) wide.

are you tired of traveling with smart outfits squished into your suitcase, making them creased and crumpled? well, this very easy-to-make suit carrier holds not only suits but also coats, dresses, blouses, and posh sweaters too! even when you aren't going anywhere, it is a great way of protecting your favorite clothes while they are hanging in the closet.

make the loop.

fold a ⅜in (1cm) hem over to the wrong side along each long edge of the fabric piece and press. then fold the fabric in half lengthwise so the two folded edges meet. press and pin. stitch along the open side, stitching as close to the edge as possible for a neat finish. backstitch at the start and finish to fasten the seam. stitch the same line along the opposite side to finish the loop.

⅜in (1cm)

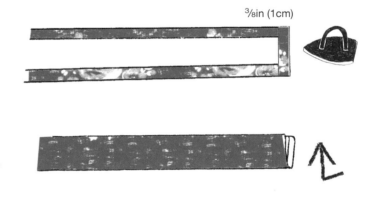

add the bias binding.
fold the front piece in half lengthwise and cut along this line. fold the bias binding in half lengthwise and press. pin the bias binding along the long straight edge of one front half, following the instructions for adding bias binding as given on page 20. repeat this on the corresponding straight edge of the second half.

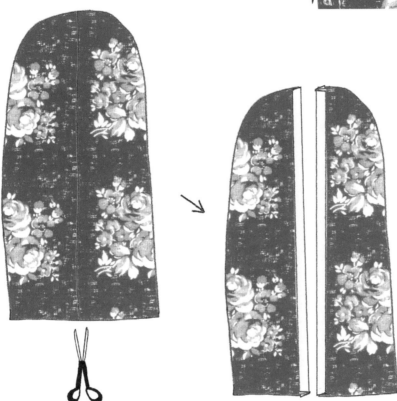

add the zipper end.
before applying the zipper, add the zipper end. place the small zipper end piece and the cut end of the zipper right sides together. stitch a ¼in (5mm) seam. fold the unstitched side of the zipper end back ⅜in (1cm), then fold the whole piece around to the back side of the zipper, being careful to keep the raw edge tucked underneath. stitch in place, sewing a little to the right of the first seam just sewn, making sure you catch the tucked side of the zipper end in as you stitch.

apply the zipper.

apply the zipper to the two front panels: the open end of the zipper needs to start at the top of the suit carrier and should line up with the top of the bound edge. pin the zipper in place along each edge in turn. the zipper should finish 4in (10cm) short of the bottom edge. then follow the instructions for applying a zip as given on page 23.

join the panels.

with right sides together, place the front and back panels with the raw edges even. the two pieces of oilcloth may stick together so it can take some time to line them up exactly. unzip the zipper to over halfway so you will be able to turn the cover right side out once stitched. pin all the way around. fold your prepared loop in half. then slot it in between the front and back panels at the center of the bottom edge, with the fold facing inward and the raw edges even. pin in place. stitch around the outside edge with a ¾in (2cm) seam, trapping in the loop as you sew. backstitch at the start and finish to fasten the seam. trim the excess seam allowance all the way around with pinking shears.

add the hanger.

turn the suit carrier right side out. fit the suit carrier over the wire hanger, taking the hanger's "neck" through the hole at the top where the zipper finishes.

now fill the carrier with your best outfits. i highly recommend having a weekend away to test your new suit carrier fully!

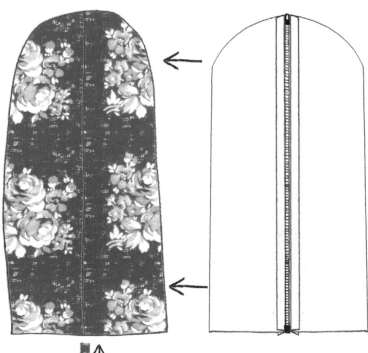

pin-tucked pillow.

things you need

1 large sheet of paper or newspaper, at least 20in x 20in (50cm x 50cm).

pencil and a length of string.

1 piece of medium-weight cotton, 20in x 60in (50cm x 150cm), for front panel.

1 piece of medium-weight canvas or cotton drill, 21in x 21in (52cm x 52cm) for back panel.

1 upholstery zipper, 20in (50cm) long.

cotton for zipper end, 1¼in x 1¾in (3cm x 4cm).

tailor's chalk.

1 feather-filled round pillow form 19in (48cm) in diameter.

pin tucking is a straightforward sewing technique, which delivers stunningly elegant results. it is a rather lengthy process, but once you have the hang of pin tucking, it is both simple and satisifying.

you can achieve countless variations in size, scale, and texture when you vary the width of the pin tucks and weight of the fabric. the lighter the weight of the fabric, the smaller the pin tucks can go, while larger, bolder, textured pin tucks can be achieved with wonderful weighty linens and vintage cottons. here I have used a tasar silk with a beautiful sheen to it, which is nice and sturdy to work with and produces a bold and gloriously textured result.

make the pattern.

the best way to do this is to use the old trick of attaching a piece of string to a pencil. measure the length of string to 10in (25cm)—half the diameter of the 20in (50cm) circle required. with one hand, hold the end of the string in the center of the sheet of paper and with the other hand pull the string taut. draw the pencil around to create a full circle. cut out the pattern and put it to one side—it will be used later to cut out the circular panels.

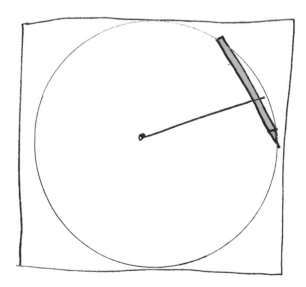

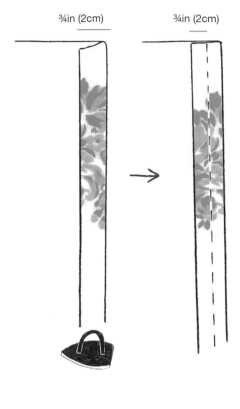

¾in (2cm)   ¾in (2cm)

make the pin-tucked panel.
you will need your iron and ironing board set up as near as possible to your sewing machine. starting at the left edge of the front panel piece, fold the fabric over by ¾in (2cm) and press. stitch a ⅜in (1cm) seam down the length of the fold. press the seam flat on the back and front and press the pin tuck to the left. (one down, lots to go!) measuring from the newly stitched line, fold the fabric again by ¾in (2cm) and press. stitch a ⅜in (1cm) seam down the length of the fold. press this on the back and front, pressing the pin tuck to the left. repeat this all the way along the fabric until you have pin tucked the lot. this takes a little time, to-ing and fro-ing from sewing machine to iron, but i actually find it quite therapeutic.

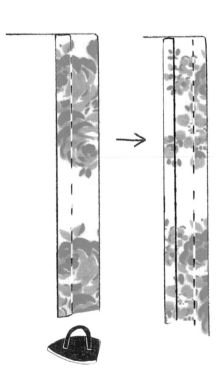

apply the zipper.

cut the back panel in half directly down the middle. fold a ⅜in (1cm) hem over to the wrong side along both newly cut straight edges. press and pin. then follow the instructions for applying a zipper as given on page 23.

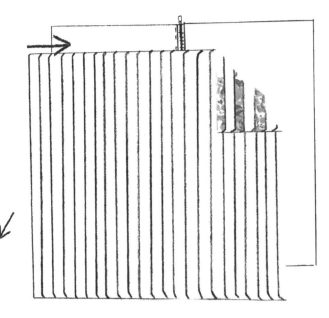

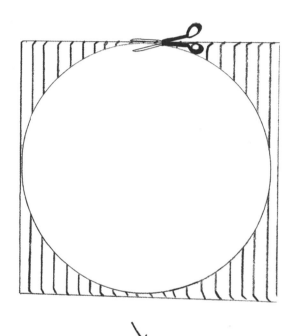

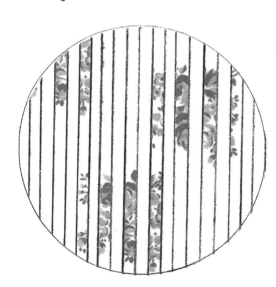

join the panels.

with right sides together, place the front and back panels with the raw edges even. place the circular pattern on top and, using tailor's chalk, trace around the pattern onto the fabric. unzip the zipper to over halfway so you will be able to turn the cover right side out once stitched. pin the panels together all the way around just inside the chalk line. cut out following the chalk line. stitch all the way around with a ⅜in (1cm) seam. backstitch at the start and finish to fasten the seam. on the curved seam, cut notches into the seam allowance. turn the pillow cover right side out and press. stuff with the feather pillow form.

note.

it is nice to vary the pin tucking here and there. it works very well if you pin tuck only two thirds of the front panel, leaving a flat area which is "untucked", as i have done on the round pillow shown on page 110. otherwise, if you prefer a square or rectangular cushion, sew straight seams instead of curved.

bedspread.

things you need

2 pieces of dupion silk, each 54in x 79in (137cm x 200cm).

1 piece of 6oz polyester batting, 54in x 79in (137cm x 200cm)—you may have to use 2 pieces to achieve this size.

2 pieces of linen for the edging, each 9½in x 80½in (24cm x 204cm) and a further 2 pieces each 9½in x 55½in (24cm x 141cm).

tailor's chalk and yardstick (optional)

draw out the grid.

you will need a large floor area or table to work on for this project: it is not difficult, but it does take up a rather large space! with wrong sides together, lay the two silk pieces on top of each other with the batting sandwiched in between. the idea is to stitch a 4in (10cm) grid all over the bedspread. this can either be sewn "by eye" creating an endearingly naïve look (one which i personally love), or for greater accuracy you can draw straight lines onto the fabric using tailor's chalk and a yardstick as a guide.

snuggling up with a hot chocolate and the sunday newspapers is a wonderful (albeit rather rare) luxury. in the winter months, layering an extra bedspread on top of a duvet or traditional blankets provides much-needed extra warmth to a bed and achieves that snug-as-a-bug-in-a-rug feeling!

stitch the grid.

hand baste all three layers together with lines of stitching 4in (10cm) apart, running lengthwise down the fabric. stitch along the rows. backstitch at the start and finish to fasten the lines of stitching. turn the bedspread 90 degrees. hand baste lines of stitching 4in (10cm) apart, running all the way across the fabric, to complete the grid. stitch along the rows. backstitch at the start and finish to fasten the lines of stitching. (see page 12 for more information on basting and stitching.) if you find the bulk of three layers of fabric too great to fit under the arm of your sewing machine, the layers can be stitched together by hand.

4in (10cm)

⅜in (1cm)

¾in (2cm)

prepare the edging.

fold a ⅜in (1cm) hem over to the wrong side along each long edge of the edging pieces and press. fold a ¾in (2cm) hem over to the wrong side at both short ends and press. then fold each piece down the middle lengthwise so the two turned edges are even. press and pin.

edge the bedspread.
starting with the two shortest edges, sandwich the stitched bedspread panel into the two shorter folded edging pieces, one on either side. pin in place and stitch. stitch as close to the turned-under edges as possible for a neat finish. backstitch at the start and finish to fasten.

finish the bedspread.
repeat this along the two longer edges using the two longer folded edging pieces. overlap the shorter edge pieces at the corners. pin in place and stitch as before. backstitch at the start and finish to fasten the seam.

fling the finished bedspread onto your freshly laundered bed. add pillows, and the daily newspaper—and relax!

for the laundry

laundry or storage bag.

things you need

1 piece of medium weight cotton or linen (I have used a medium weight plain weave cotton), 60in x 24in (150cm x 60cm).

2 lengths of cotton cord, each 48in (120cm) long, for drawstring ties.

1 large safety pin or diaper pin.

keep your dirty laundry in order until wash day in a fabulous handmade bag. it is also extremely useful for storing a million other things—shoe polish, babies' bits and pieces, soap flakes, socks and undies...

the instructions here are for a laundry bag, but using this method you can make a bag to any size you like depending what you need it for. simply scale the measurements given either up or down proportionally.

prepare the cord casing.

measure 3in (8cm) in from each end of the fabric piece and make a cut of ½in (1cm) at each corner as shown to create a flap.

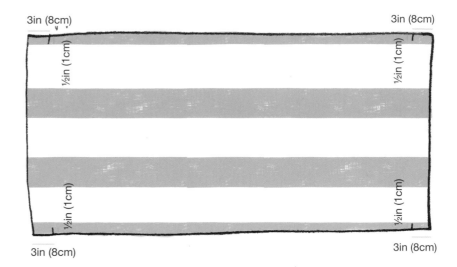

stitch the cord casing.

fold each cord casing flap over to the wrong side by ¼in (5mm). press. fold again by a further ¼in (5mm) to enclose the raw edge. press. pin and stitch. backstitch at the start and finish to fasten the seam.

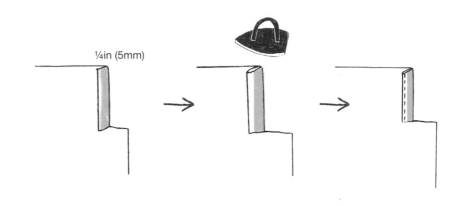

finish the cord casing.

fold a ¼in (5mm) hem over to the wrong side along each short end. press. then fold the short edges over to the wrong side again so they are level with the ½in (1cm) cut previously made in the fabric. press. pin and stitch in place. stitch as close to the edges as possible for a neat finish. backstitch at the start and finish to fasten.

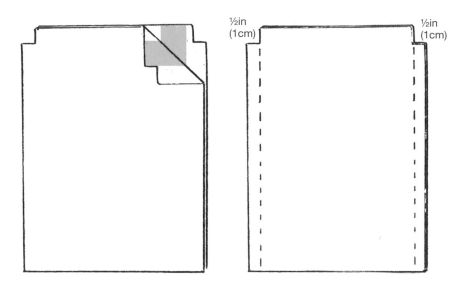

½in (1cm)   ½in (1cm)

stitch the bag.
with right sides together, fold the whole fabric piece in half so the raw edges meet as shown. pin the side edges together. stitch both edges with a ½in (1cm) seam. trim the excess seam allowance all the way around with pinking shears.

finish the bag.
turn the bag right side out and press the seams. cut the cotton cord in half and attach one end of each piece to a large safety pin (if you can get your hands on one, an old-fashioned diaper pin is best for this). thread the two cords all the way through both sides of the cord casing. when fully threaded, and holding onto both ends of the cords, gently pull one of the ends to determine which cord is which, and fasten each cord separately with a secure knot. to finish pull one of the knotted cords through to the opposite side of the casing so you end up with a knot at either side, making it super easy to draw the strings together when you need to close the bag.

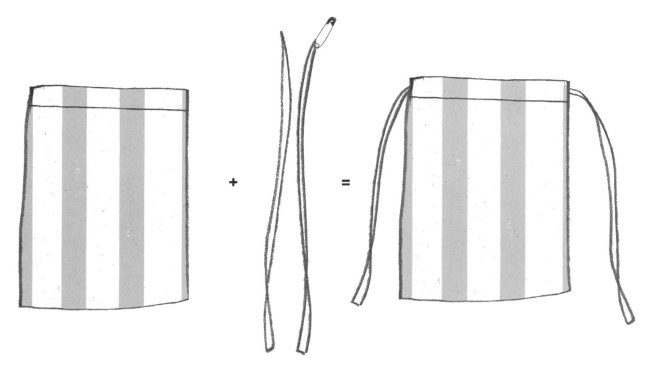

clothespin bag

things you need

1 piece of medium weight cotton canvas, 16in x 32in (40cm x 80cm).

2 lengths of bias binding, each 20in (50cm) long.

2 lengths of cotton cord, each 8in (20cm) long, for ties.

1 length of square wooden dowel, ¾in x ¾in x 15in (1.8cm x 1.8cm x 38cm).

1 metal screw hook (one taken from an old wooden coat hanger is ideal).

why not hang out your washing in style with a homemade clothespin bag. a stripe or floral print fabric with contrast binding works excellently for this project. wooden clothespins are a must-have!

add the bias binding and ties.
fold each strip of bias binding in half lengthwise and pin in place over the short edges of the canvas. with the fabric face up, at the center of each bound edge slot a cord tie underneath the bias binding. pin in place. stitch as close to the turned edge of the binding as possible, taking care to catch the underside of the binding as you sew and to secure the ties; for extra strength make a double stitch over each tie. tuck the raw edge of the binding under for a neat finish at each end.

sew the side seams.
with right sides together, fold the canvas so the bound edges meet one third of the way down from the top. pin and stitch the sides with ⅜in (1cm) seams. backstitch at the start and finish to fasten the seams.

add the hook and dowel.
turn the bag right side out and press. slip the dowel inside the bag at the top, to fit snugly. with tailor's chalk, mark the center point along the top edge. screw the hook into the dowel through the fabric at this point.

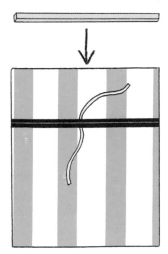

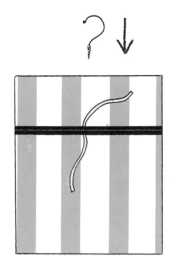

the bag is now ready to fill with clothespins!

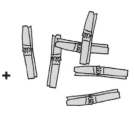

plastic bag holder.

things you need

1 disk of medium weight cotton or linen, 5½in (14cm) in diameter, for base.

1 piece of medium weight cotton or linen, 16in x 24½in (40cm x 62cm).

1 length of cotton cord, 40in (100cm) long, for drawstring ties.

2 lengths of bias binding, each 6¼in (16cm) long.

1 large safety pin or diaper pin.

do your bit for the environment by making sure you recycle any plastic bags that you pick up on shopping trips. this snazzy homemade holder keeps plastic bags neat, tidy, and ready to reuse.

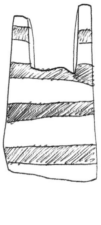

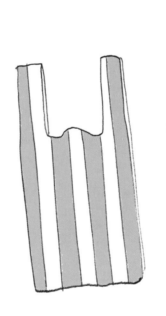

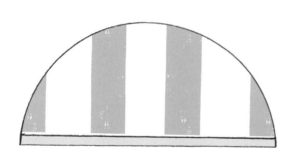

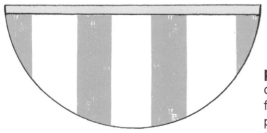

prepare the base.
cut the cotton disk in half directly down the middle. fold each strip of bias binding in half lengthwise and pin in place over the straight edges. stitch as close to the turned-under edge of the binding as possible, taking care to catch the underside of the binding as you sew. tuck the raw edge of the binding under for a neat finish at each end.

prepare the cord casing.

measure 3in (8cm) in from one end of the fabric piece and make a cut of ½in (1cm) at both corners as shown to create a flap.

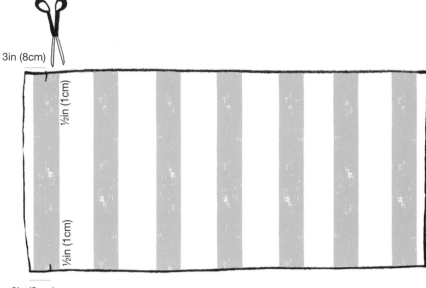

3in (8cm)

½in (1cm)

½in (1cm)

3in (8cm)

stitch the cord casing ends.

fold each cord casing flap over to the wrong side by ¼in (5mm). press. fold again by a further ¼in (5mm) to enclose the raw edge. press. pin and stitch. backstitch at the start and finish to fasten the seam.

¼in (5mm)

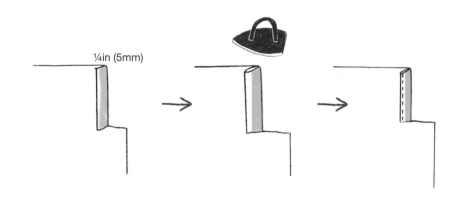

¼in (5mm)

finish the cord casing.

fold a ¼in (5mm) hem over to the wrong side along each short end. press. then fold the short edges over to the wrong side again so they are level with the ½in (1cm) cut previously made in the fabric. press. pin and stitch in place. stitch as close to the edges as possible for a neat finish. backstitch at the start and finish to fasten.

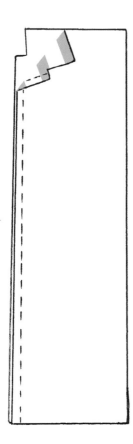

stitch the holder.
with right sides together, fold the whole fabric piece in half lengthwise so the raw edges meet as shown. pin the edges together. stitch the side with a ½in (1cm) seam.

fit the base.
prepare the main piece for fitting the base by making a round of ½in (1cm) cuts, ¾in (2cm) apart, at each end. with the bound edges of the two base pieces butted up together, pin the base in place. stitch a ⅝in (1.5cm) seam around the base. this is a little tricky so take your time: if you need to add a little pleat here and there to make it fit, then do. backstitch at the start and finish to fasten.

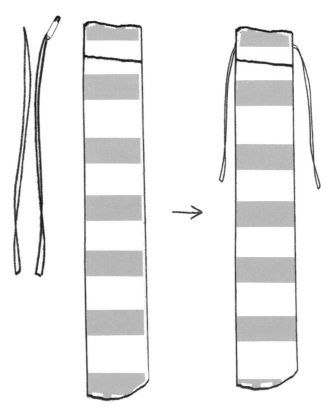

finish the holder.
turn the bag right side out and press the seams. cut the cotton cord in half and attach one end of each piece to a large safety or diaper pin. thread the two cords all the way through both sides of the cord casing. when fully threaded, and holding onto both ends of the cords, gently pull one of the ends to determine which cord is which, and fasten each cord separately with a secure knot. to finish pull one of the knotted cords through to the opposite side of the casing so you end up with a knot at either side, making it super easy to draw the strings together when you need to close the holder.

now fill your holder with plastic bags!

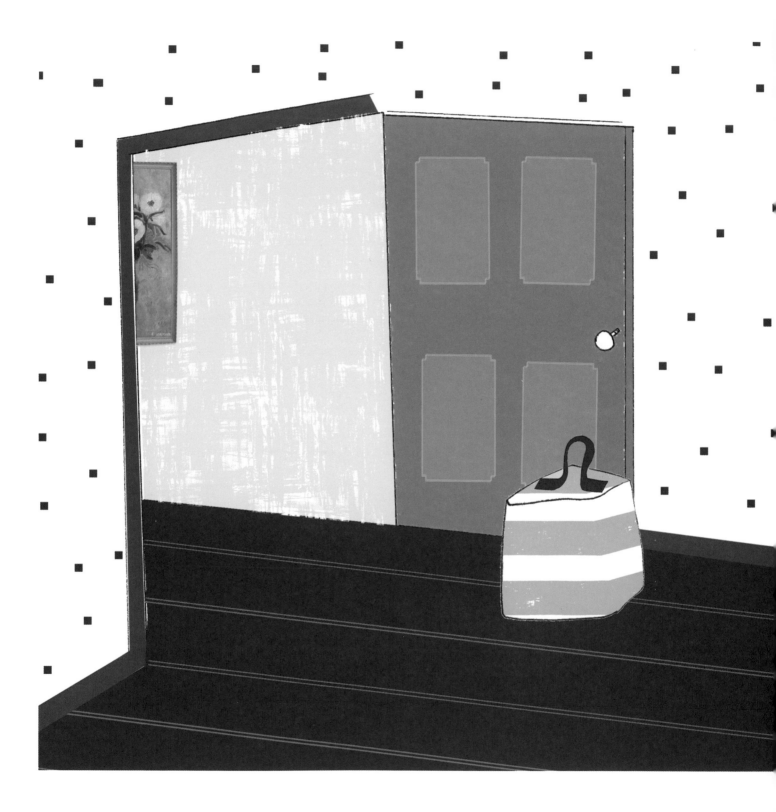

doorstop.

things you need

2 pieces of medium or heavyweight cotton, 6¾in x 6¾in (17cm x 17cm), for the base and lid.

1 piece of medium or heavyweight cotton, 24¾in x 8in (62cm x 20cm), for the main body.

1 piece of medium or heavyweight cotton, 8¾in x 2¼in (22cm x 6cm), for the handle.

1 large plastic freezer bag or similar.

1 rubber band.

a small amount of sand, rice, or similar for filling.

this handy little doorstop, in all its homemade glory, is a classic design; simple to make, it will prevent your doors from slamming. a medium to heavyweight cotton is the best fabric to use for this project.

make the handle.
fold a ³/₈in (1cm) hem over to the wrong side along all four sides of the fabric piece and press. then fold the fabric in half lengthwise so the turned edges meet. press and pin. stitch together all the way around, stitching as close to the edge as possible for a neat finish. backstitch at the start and finish to fasten the seam.

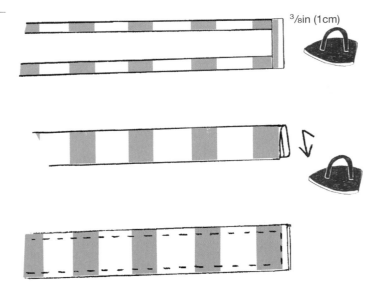

³/₈in (1cm)

add the handle.

on the right side of the lid piece position the ends of the handle as shown. pin in place. stitch the handle to the doorstop lid; for extra strength stitch a rectangle and then add a cross in the middle.

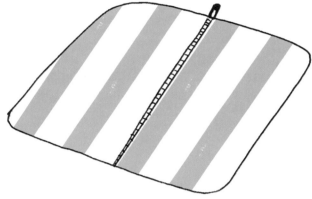

apply the zipper.

cut the base piece in half down the middle. fold a ⅜in (1cm) hem over to the wrong side along both newly cut edges. press and pin. then follow the instructions for applying a zipper as given on page 23. put to one side.

stitch the body.

with right sides together, fold the main body in half crosswise so the raw edges meet as shown. pin the edges together. stitch the short side with a ⅜in (1cm) seam. press the seam flat.

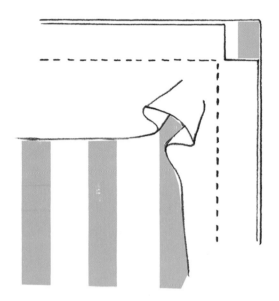

join all the pieces.

with right sides together, pin the main body to the base piece. clip the corners to achieve a neat finish. (make sure the zipper is open for the next part as you will need to get a hand in to turn the doorstop right side out once you have finished stitching.) following the instructions for sewing boxed corners as given on page 18, stitch the main body in place with one continuous seam, taking a $^3/_8$in (1cm) seam. backstitch at the start and finish to fasten the seam. repeat this process to join the main body to the lid piece. turn the doorstop right side out and press the seams (the edge of the ironing board helps with this).

line and fill the doorstop.

line the doorstop with the plastic freezer bag. fill the bag with sand, rice, or other chosen filling; during filling, give the doorstop a few vigorous shakes to ensure it is filled to its maximum. twist the opening of the plastic bag together and secure with a rubber band. zip up the doorstop and it is ready to use.

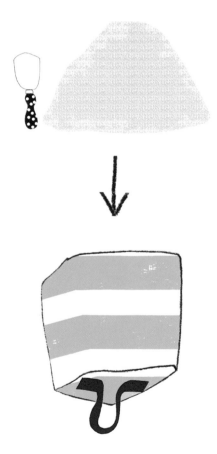

shoe bag.

things you need

2 pieces of medium weight cotton, 15in x 18in (38cm x 46cm).

1 piece of medium weight cotton, 9½in x 4¾in (24cm x 12cm).

1 closed-end zipper, 16in (40cm) long.

i find these little shoe bags extremely useful, especially when traveling. they are great for when you need to pack shoes into your suitcase, neatly and cleanly protecting both your shoes and your clothes. they are also great for popping sneakers into, whether for a game of tennis or a jog after work!

make the loop.
fold a ³⁄₈in (1cm) hem over to the wrong side along all four sides of the smaller fabric piece and press. then fold the fabric in half lengthwise so the folded edges meet. press and pin. stitch together all the way around, stitching as close to the edge as possible for a neat finish. backstitch at the start and finish to fasten the seam.

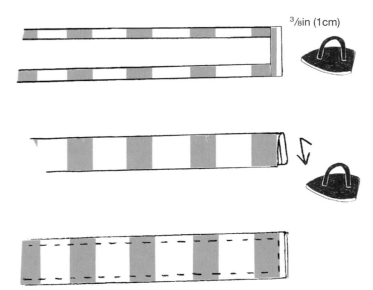

³⁄₈in (1cm)

apply the zipper.

fold a ^{3}/8in (1cm) hem over to the wrong side along one short end of both the two main cotton pieces. press and pin. then follow the instructions for applying a zipper as given on page 23.

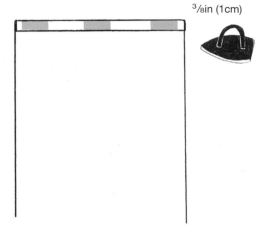

^{3}/8in (1cm)

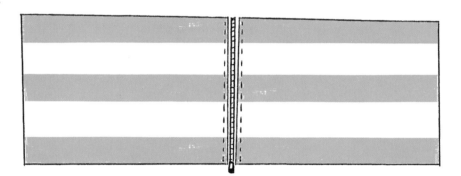

stitch the bag.

pin the other two short edges, with right sides together. stitch a ^{3}/8in (1cm) seam. press the seam flat. turn the bag right side out. (the bag is finished with french seams along the sides, so there is no danger of fluffing your suede shoes with any raw fabric edges inside.) then position the bag so that the zipper sits 3in (8cm) down from the top edge and so the raw edges meet as shown. pin the edges together. stitch the sides with ^{3}/8in (1cm) seams, making sure the zipper is half open. trim the seam allowance back to ¼in (5mm). turn the bag wrong side out again.

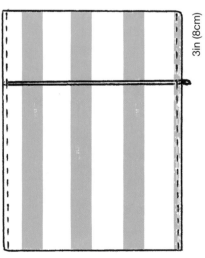

3in (8cm)

^{3}/8in (1cm)

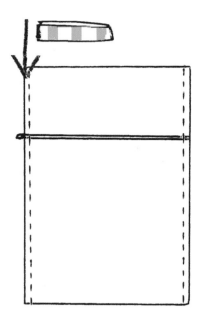

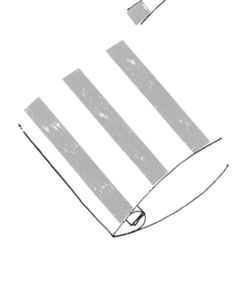

add the loop and complete the bag.

with the bag wrong side out and the zipped front face up, tuck the folded loop inside the bag at the top left-hand corner so the raw edges of the loop butt up to the inside seam. pin in place. then stitch down each side with a ⅝in (1.5cm) seam, enclosing the raw edges in the french seam as you sew (see page 17), taking care to secure the loop; for extra strength make a double stitch over the loop. turn the bag right side out and press to finish.

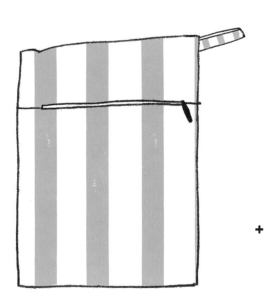

+

templates.

not in the same scale.
each square of each grid
represents 2in x 2in (5cm
x 5cm).

egg cozy (see pages 38–9).

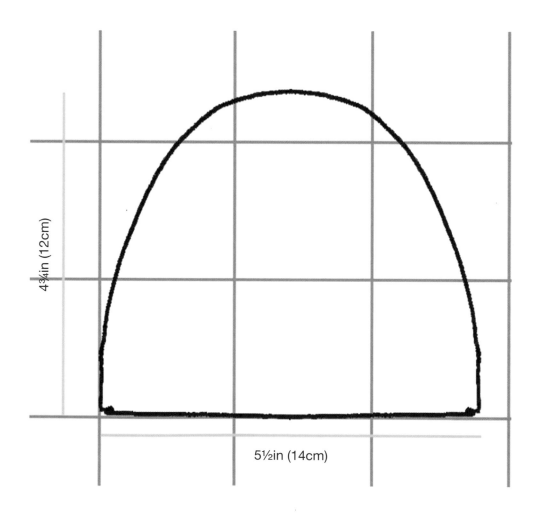

4¾in (12cm)

5½in (14cm)

apron (see pages 40–1).

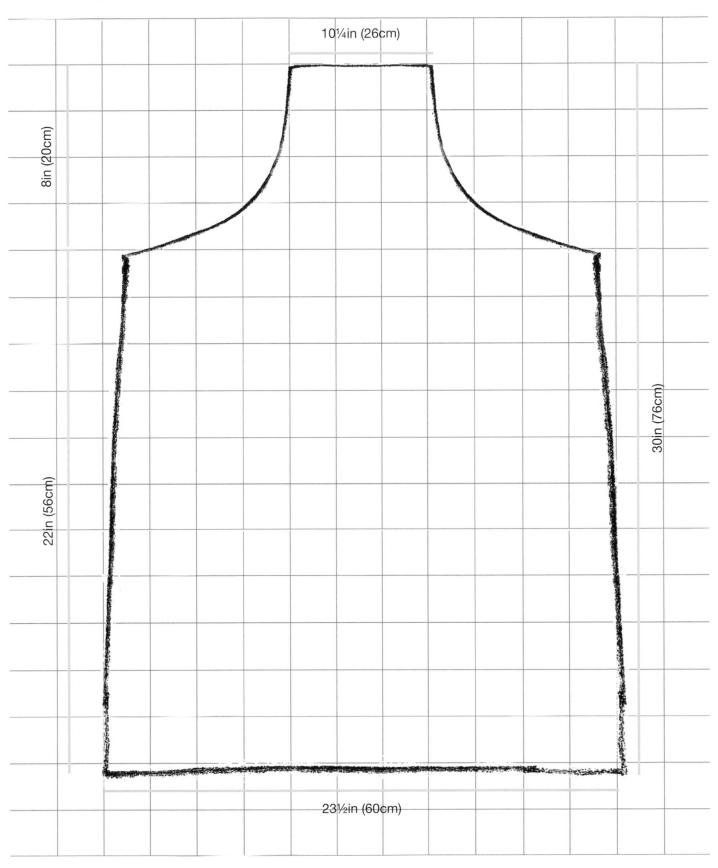

10¼in (26cm)

8in (20cm)

30in (76cm)

22in (56cm)

23½in (60cm)

**hanger coat
(see pages 104–5).**

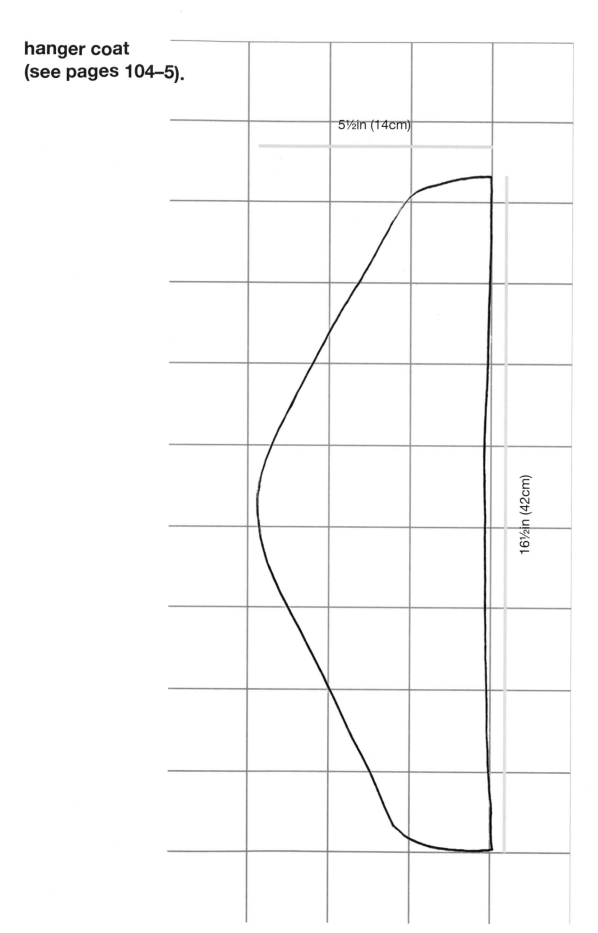

5½in (14cm)

16½in (42cm)

**suit carrier
(see pages 106–9).**

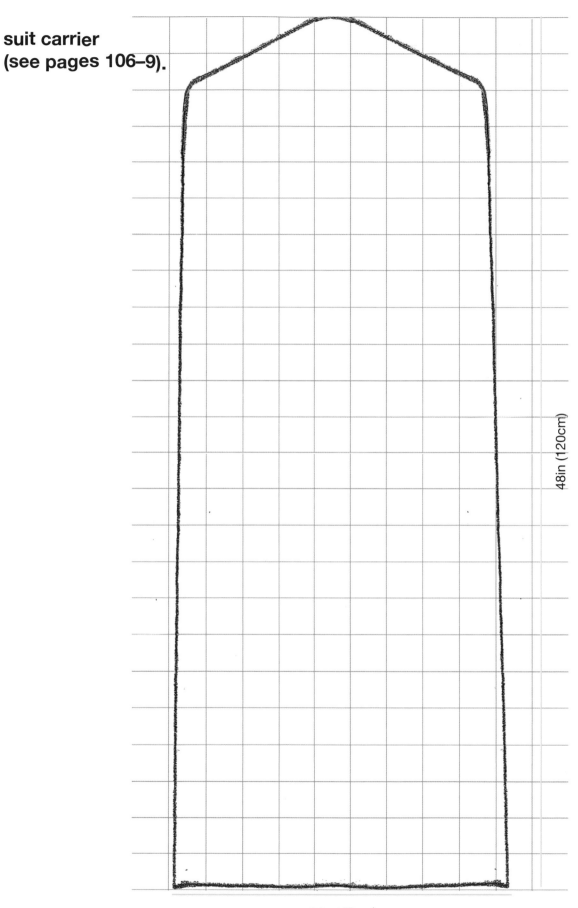

48in (120cm)

17in (43cm)

hot-water bottle cover (see pages 96–9).

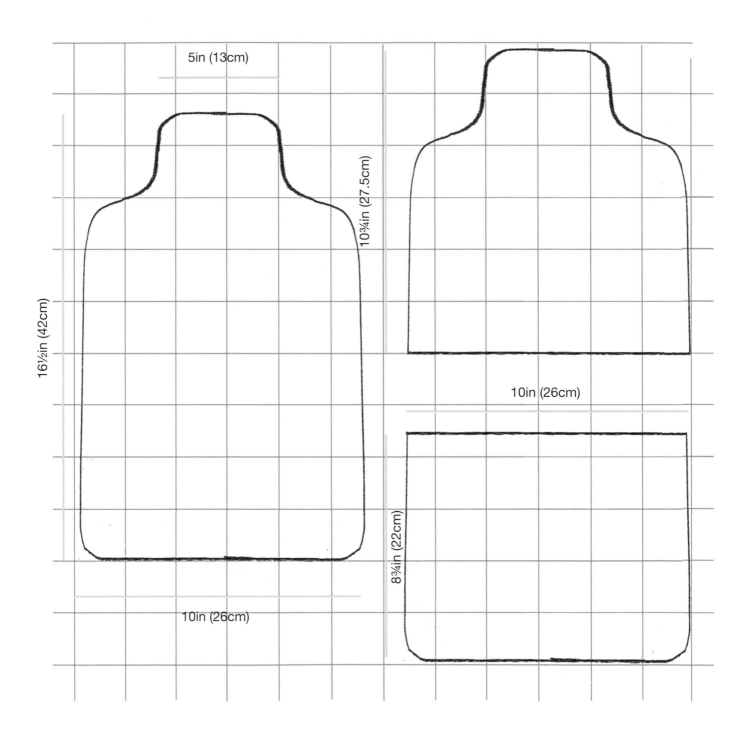

5in (13cm)

10¾in (27.5cm)

16½in (42cm)

10in (26cm)

10in (26cm)

8¾in (22cm)

acknowledgments.

many, many thanks to the following people whose generous support, encouragement, and input over the past few months have helped to make this book possible.

to jane, lisa, and claire for their support and expertise. to katie, the super stylist and superior spellchecker, for her total understanding of my vision and wondrous encouragement. to ben for the fantastic photography and portrait patience. to mum, dad, and anna for their unconditional support, love, and belief in me, which goes far beyond this book. also to mum for her extensive roadtesting, instruction checking, and telephone encyclopedia-type advice. to sally and glyn for the piles of 1960s sewing patterns, inspirational books, and much encouragement. to jo for her support, belief, drive, and sheer determination every day. martha, emma, kangan, debbie, and victor for wide-ranging brainstorming, encouragement, roadtesting, cups of tea, and general marvelousness. and to rich, every day for his unconditional support, encouragement, and love, my rock.

lisa stickley london
74 landor road
london sw9 9ph
UK
tel +44 (0)20 7737 8067
www.lisastickleylondon.com